Taking Responsibility for the Life of Complex Human Ecosystems

Taking Responsibility for the Life of Complex Human Ecosystems

Deep Accountability

By Gary R. Gunderson and James R. Cochrane

A

ANTHEM PRESS

Anthem Press
An imprint of Wimbledon Publishing Company
www.anthempress.com

This edition first published in UK and USA 2025
by ANTHEM PRESS
75–76 Blackfriars Road, London SE1 8HA, UK
or PO Box 9779, London SW19 7ZG, UK
and
244 Madison Ave #116, New York, NY 10016, USA

British Library Cataloguing-in-Publication Data
A catalogue record for this book is available from the British Library.

Library of Congress Control Number: 2025938884

ISBN-13: 978-1-83999-533-0 (Hbk)
ISBN-10: 1-83999-533-5 (Hbk)
ISBN-13: 978-1-83999-534-7 (Pbk)
ISBN-10: 1-83999-534-3 (Pbk)

Cover Credit: *'Zwischen den Zeiten und Krieg'* acrylic painting on canvas by
Hildegard Brand

This title is also available as an eBook.

CONTENTS

ACKNOWLEDGEMENTS

More than most, this book reflects deep conversations with many people over a lengthy span of time. Some key ideas – such as 'deep accountability' or 'the leading causes of life' – are ours, but we also act in many ways as editors of ideas that arise from many other people.

The Scots may head for the pub for life-giving conversation, but we head for the Fellows of the Leading Causes of Life Initiative (LCLI). What you will read in this book owes a great deal to free-flowing conversations with them, including at a five-day gathering in Greyton, later another at Goedgedacht Farm, both near Cape Town. Through laughter, tears and intense dialogue, we there tested the ideas behind the various chapters with many Fellows, including Matthew Bersagel Braley, Sarah Crawford-Browne, Teresa Cutts, Marcellino Jonas, Bastienne Klein, Horst Kleinschmidt, Michael Lapsley, Sandy Lazarus, Leslie London, Tyler Norris, Jill Olivier, Doug Reeler, Beulah Tertiens-Reeler, Arvind Singhal, Deon Snyman and Craig Stewart.

Feeding into this over time have been many conversations elsewhere with other Fellows of the LCLI. They include Sunny Anand, Dora Barilla, Kevin Barnett, Elias Bongmba, Heidi Christensen, Thandeka Cochrane, Nomvula Dlamini, Doug Easterling, Shirley Fleming, Tor Haugstad, Ellen Idler, Maria Jones, Evance Kalula, Mosi Kisare, Paul Laurienti, Andy McCarroll, Doug McGaughey, Bobby Milstein, Jeremy Moseley, Tobias Müller, Shingai Ndinga, Kirsten Peachey, Tom Petersen, Larry Pray, Monte Roulier, Aziz Royesh, Somava Saha, Steve Scoggin, Mohamed Seedat, Geordan Shannon, Fred Smith, Naiema Taliep, Marlese von Broembsen, Emily Viverette, Terry Williams, Francis Wilson, Jerry Winslow and Heather Wood Ion (for a full listing of Fellows, see: www.leading-causes.com/lcl-fellows---list.html).

Many other people from various walks of life and disciplines also shape our thoughts and work. Some are no longer with us in body, but their spirit and friendship continue to inspire and motivate us. Among those who have had a direct impact on our lives and thoughts are for Gary: Bill Foege, Jimmy Carter and Jim Curran, who opened up extraordinary space for this work at The Carter Centre, and later Gary Shorb and John McConnell did the same in Memphis and North Carolina. For Jim, it includes Theo Kotze and Beyers Naudé of the banned Christian Institute of Southern Africa, Steve Biko, Robert Sobukwe, Alex Boraine, Martha Snyder, Ross Snyder and Ted Jennings.

We thank, too, the leaders and colleagues of the healthcare systems in Memphis and Winston-Salem, and the broad learning networks of Stakeholder Health (now Hold.Health), colleagues at the National Academies of Sciences Roundtable on Population Health, and in earlier days, the inspiring team of people who built the African Religious Health Assets Programme. We also name Tom Peterson in Little Rock, Arkansas, and local friends on the reality of the ground of Winston-Salem in North Carolina, of Tübingen in Germany and of Cape Town in South Africa.

Gary notes that without his wife, love and best colleague, Dr Teresa Cutts, almost nothing of his would ever find daylight, much less print. Jim, in turn, gains from the much more practical and grounded work of his spouse, Renate, in the field of HIV and AIDS in southern Africa and in recovering the history of the persecution and murder of members of Jewish families who lived in the German village in which she grew up as a pastor's daughter.

Spouses and children put up with a great deal from authors. Both families are rich in grace and fortitude, but not as observers. They have helped us think – and more importantly – *live* through these days. Son, daughters and wives who are also colleagues and friends teach us about generous generativity and remind us of what it means to be deeply accountable for the life we live.

Chapter 1

NOW

Everest shrinking, ocean rising – profound changes taking place that should be imperceptible to humans watching on a smartphone newsfeed. How to live amid these and other tumbling certainties? Our friend Daniel Taylor is at home in the highest reaches of the tallest mountains in Nepal, pillars that reach into the jet stream as it whips past the peaks. While we were still writing this book, he went back to the lofty villages where his dad and he had long lived and walked, where he had over time solved the mystery of the Yeti[1] and where he had helped persuade Nepal, Tibet and China to create three national parks around Mount Everest. Now back on the mountain, he hoped to complete a personal journey, a circle of discovery he had spent decades exploring about how lasting change emerges, and how it is sustained over time. It was not to be.

After reaching a high glacier, he found it covered several feet deep in a crazy quilt of new boulders, released by the permafrost melting at elevations never anticipated before. Indeed, he had to shelter in caves during the day as the mountain fell around him. This land has always been dynamic but at a tectonic pace – a slow catastrophe as the Indian tectonic plate continues to move north, diving below the Himalayan plateau, raising it even higher into the sky, the friction building over decades until it predictably releases some of the most severe earthquakes on the planet. Dan'l watched hundreds of monasteries levelled in 2015.

What Dan'l saw now was not caused by the rising of the tectonic plates but something more like a planetary death rattle, the climate melting snow and ice quicker than even the highest mountains could withstand. Unable to go back to the villages of his youth where he had since sought to map sustainable change, Dan'l called for rescue by a brave helicopter pilot in the short window after dawn before boulders spat down onto the trails once more.

Who could imagine the Himalayas falling apart? But then who could imagine 90 degrees Fahrenheit on the northern Arctic coast of Alaska? Or ice shelves the size of nations breaking off in Antarctica at the other end of the planet? Boreal forests turning into firestorms? Hurricanes so regularly severe we need new measures? Extinctions accelerating at a rate unknown since the dinosaurs left town?

Equally, who could imagine battle tanks, cluster bombs and missiles raining down on European land in Ukraine only a generation removed from the 'never again' wars, or violence erupting like a spewing volcano in Palestine/Israel, in Myanmar, in Tigray, in Sudan, in far too many places, with threats of more to come? The United States Capitol under violent siege, an impossible act defended by people sworn to protect dialogue and deliberation – and then the next election voting in the instigator-in-chief? Nearly the entire miraculous South African miracle of a peaceful end of Apartheid desecrated by the most venal and brazen kind of state capture?[2] The impossible concentration of wealth in a handful of impossibly rich human lives and a new Feudalism delighting a few while hundreds of millions have no clean water to drink or a place to defecate ('Let them eat tweets')?

We may be in the last tragic era of our young species. We are only a few generations into the period marked by what we may now call the Anthropocene.[3] We broke the world, it's ours now, and as we see the collapse underway, we realize our fundamental human impact on the complex human ecosystems. Maybe the humbling gives us hope that we might yet act responsibly. We will need more than humility, though; we need to be deeply accountable for our presence in the world. That is what this compact book is about.

To be sure, some of us humans are perplexed, others enraged, others in denial, while still others seek to build protected enclaves for themselves to keep it all at bay.[4] Do we choose fight or flight, delay or attack? How do we know when there is nobody to fight with whom we are not deeply entangled and on whom our life does not depend? Some think innovative technologies and masses of finance will do the trick. Perhaps a few of us can start again on Mars or the Moon, but the other 99.9 per cent of us have nowhere else to go at all.

It should then be no surprise that the anger of the younger generations moves towards fury as the cost of our naiveté and the failure of our responsibility becomes clear. The young see that what sometimes looks like naiveté is instead cynical, not ignorant. The comfortably old do not have the time or energy to make the choices that would give the young a chance. Even those of us older ones who imagine ourselves allies have acted at a leisurely pace even as the boulders rain down.

This is perhaps easily explainable psychologically and sociologically. It is hard to respond to tectonic phenomena with our small human words and limited tools. Yet what parent would waste another day scattering their energies on this and that incomplete and incoherent action before it all comes down on our children and their children? Won't our children wonder in their deepening distress what we did to give them a chance while beauty, hope and compassion were still possible? How are we to grasp the totality so that we act in ways that lead to life? This is why this book, and the Fellows who helped shape it, ask how we can be *deeply accountable* in investing our relative handful of years, our small weight of influence, our inherent capacities to choose, to act and to move against the abyss. What could be more important?

To approach that work, we need to think more radically, not just about the problems as they stand, but about how we are to go *beyond* them to what might be possible and tractable. We have no time for thoughtlessness. How do we humans think at all about anything, however? To comprehend our experience, we must add relevant and useful concepts to it. That requires language. Languages are malleable, and concepts in one often have no direct equivalent in another. Our concern is not that. It is language that is too limited, inadequate or misleading, reflecting a limited, inadequate or misleading grasp of experience and, thus, limited, inadequate or misleading action. Language and action are, in this view, integrally related. As Paul Ricoeur puts it, 'human action is an open work, the meaning of which is "in suspense". It is because it "opens up" new references and receives fresh relevance from them, that human deeds are also waiting for fresh interpretations which decide their meaning.'[5]

Ricoeur has also paid close attention to the power of metaphors to configure and reconfigure our actions in the world.[6] Humans live and find their way through stories built on thinking tools called metaphors. A bad metaphor (such as 'we think like computers') makes us dumb, ensures bad choices and can get us killed. A good metaphor helps us see reality and each other clearly so that we may live more fully. It's not entirely wrong to say that the fundamental tools of leaders, those responsible for the thousands of choices that lead to life or collapse, are words and images.

On 24 June 2021, at approximately 1:22 a.m. EDT, as Wikipedia summarizes it, a 12-storey beachfront condominium in the Miami suburb of Surfside, Florida, United States, partially collapsed, causing the deaths of 98 people;[7] this included the wife of a close friend of Gary's, who had been a hospital CEO. There are thousands of similar condos around the world. If you have someone you love living in one of them next to a rising tide, you pray that the architects, engineers, contractors, welders and finally, the inspectors not only did their job but were guided by timely science, itself guided by the relevant metaphors. One is climate change, a metaphor that has become a battlefield. Who would think the design of an apartment building, as the salt penetrates and defeats the welds holding everything up, would also need all of them to take climate change into account? If we do not think with the correct thinking tools, the building will collapse.

As the biblical tradition has it (influenced by Platonism), words are really all God had at the start ('In the beginning was the word'). This reflects what we as human beings also do in creating anything; we begin with an idea, an image, like a seed of the future. These word-seeds, these metaphors, hold within them a tightly compressed ensemble of ideas about what is possible, by which we make or create new realities. Leaders build on metaphors. The most dangerous are the ones they hold so closely they can't see them. An out-dated metaphor will kill those for whom you are responsible. Even your best work will fall down if built on wrong intellectual ground. This is why in this time when the oceans rise, tundra burns and social norms shred, we write this slender book for those in a position to make the decisions that will lead us to life or death.

Metaphors, then, are not just bits of language that are tools. Not the hammer that strikes the nail; they are the tool that makes the hammer. Perhaps they are more like a trellis on which our thoughts grow. Playing with them is serious business with significant practical implications for how we act and think. Key metaphors function to open up our language to unexpected ways of seeing that are simultaneously different ways of being/becoming, redirecting our action. Equally, when established metaphors become ossified, archaic, habitual or mere slogans, then they are what Ricoeur calls dead metaphors, clichés that no longer serve their purpose.

In urgent times, it seems obvious to leap right into urgent doing. Although we are writers, we also know something about the doing. We know through chastening experience that it is crucial to start with careful language before wasting energy on useless leaping. Getting the language right is not separate from action. It is the first act grounded in experience, our first instruction: 'Experience tells us what is, but not that it must be necessarily as it is, and not otherwise.'[8] To go beyond 'what is' requires thoughtful imagination. Imagination itself needs context and coherence as a lens on where to go, what to do and how.

One of the currently more dominant or dangerous metaphors is a somewhat mechanical, computer-based one of networks to understand human cooperative activity. It leaves us tangled up in metaphorical wires that hide human complexity and make it harder to move towards human possibilities. We prefer the metaphor of a trellis or, better, a *meshwork* (see Chapter 5), which describes the many ways we are thoroughly entangled in knots of relations, subjective and objective, that thicken or unravel as we journey through life. Congruent with this is another metaphor that helps us understand our own lives and actions better: The astonishing subterranean mycelial webs that traverse the earth, and from which emerge innumerable fruits (mushrooms), some good, some poisonous. Both these metaphors help us see our reality

– especially our relationships – in ways that can help us make better choices on behalf of those we love.

In what follows, we explain all of this and offer further connected metaphors for thinking clearly. Some of these thinking tools will be surprisingly different from what you might expect, others combined in surprising ways. Each chapter brings forward a perspective that seems to fit our hands and the challenges we face. Taken together, as they should be, they build upon each other, weaving a pattern of possibilities, first of imagination, second of action.

It's not illusionary to believe that, together, we can achieve more than we might imagine. Paul Hawken, writing in *Blessed Unrest* in 2008,[9] estimated that by then two million non-governmental organizations had emerged over a few decades, each finding its way to lay hands on, and lend energy to, some hopeful possibility. The pace and urgency of that creative activity have only swelled since he wrote. Today almost every significant issue has attracted hundreds, if not thousands, of life-seeking organizational energies. In the most preposterous and unlikely places, hopeful energy is finding voice and creating traction. We are not asked to be deeply accountable for something that isn't possible. *Everything we hope for is already happening.*

We do not write, then, at the beginning of anything. The boulders are already raining down and, in many places, the social contract is increasingly up for grabs. We must pick up the pace of our work, taking responsibility for our intentions, being deeply accountable for bringing to maturity the millions of hopeful things that all over the place are trying to emerge. Perhaps you are already part of it. If so, we seek to give you reason to accelerate and deepen what you feel is calling you to do what is good and right, to give your life to life. Not in any random, desperate way but using an array of strategies that make your efforts part of a wider and vital pattern, filled with moral passion in giving life a chance at the same scale as the wounding, death-dealing threats we know almost too much about.

In short, we are not trying to outrun the boulders or cool the Arctic. We are looking directly at the profound challenges, but with a new set of lenses that help us see ourselves as part of a Great Turning – a turning towards life. Things are not just breaking down; they are also breaking open. We want you to sense that the quickening forces that threaten collapse may be matched, maybe more so, by an accelerating mesh of generative movements. We not only must, but we can use our most powerful human capacities to make the choices that lead to life, not just away from death.

We have been helped in this by a small but globally linked web of thinkers-doers, fellows in the Leading Causes of Life Initiative,[10] each enmeshed in other vital webs speaking different dialects of hope. Some are rooted in the health sciences or other academic disciplines, some in community development, some in law and finance, some in faith communities and others in public institutions. All are tethered to each other, however, by the idea that life not only *can* find a way but that it *is* finding a way, and that staring only at the dark peril is to miss where life is breaking through. Each might be an amateur in other fields, but all are also grown-ups who have worked in many contexts and across disciplinary fields. We know that too much is colonized by a restricted set of ideas and thoughts captive to the present, even when one is considering innovation or thinking about the future. This has practical implications for how we act and towards the ends we choose to act.

The metaphorical thinking tools we offer in this book help shape our way of seeing, the narratives we construct and the ends towards which we act. Some of the metaphors you will encounter are old but neglected, some mis-interpreted and some that we need probably missing. What you will read is how important our power is of 'making and unmaking' our world; you will be tasked to rethink what we mean by joy or celebration; you will meet Nemesis, the goddess of justice and retribution; you will be confronted with the importance of 'valuing everything of value'. You will encounter the term 'involution', different from evolution, linked to an understanding of complex human ecosystems,[11] which then brings us to the final chapters, on imagina-tive 'ways of walking'; on the crucial question of the 'ends that matter'; and the 'theatre of the soul' that motivates us to live up to the highest of which we are capable as human beings.

All of these thinking tools help us be less afraid of the complexity of the raining boulders and rising tides to which we must respond. We need, and can find, what we call *deep* accountability – taking responsibility for what we are capable of as human beings within whatever sphere of society or set of relationships we find ourselves. This is the opposite of grim duty. It is where we find our joy as we are meant to live. Not moved by fear, we are captured by possibilities, emergent and vital, filled with beauty and awe, calling us to become deeply accountable for what we intend and how we act. We thus share a bold urgency to craft or hone ideas worthy of our struggle for life, undergirded with a framework of coherent thought that makes our actions more likely to succeed.

After typing together for two decades about the structures and institutions of living human systems, we offer up the gift of better thinking tools, better metaphors and invite you to unwrap the gift. Completing this manuscript around Christmastime, we are quite aware that the gifts given and received may not be useful. You will know.

Notes

1 Daniel C. Taylor, *Yeti: The Ecology of a Mystery* (Oxford University Press, 2017).

2 Ivor Chipkin et al., *Shadow State: The Politics of State Capture* (Wits University Press, 2018).

3 The International Union of Geological Sciences has decided not to apply the term 'Anthropocene' to a new geological age, but it notes that the term will nonetheless 'remain an invaluable descriptor of human impact on the earth system'; see Raymond Zhong, 'Geologists Make It Official: We're Not in an "Anthropocene" Epoch', *New York Times*, 20 March 2024, https://www.nytimes.com/2024/03/20/climate/anthro-pocene-vote-upheld.html.

4 Guthrie Schrimgeour, 'Inside Mark Zuckerberg's Top-Secret Hawaii Compound', *Wired Magazine*, 14 December 2023, https://www.wired.com/story/mark-zuckerberg-inside-hawaii-compound.

5 Paul Ricoeur, *Hermeneutics and the Human Sciences* (Cambridge University Press, 1981), 208.

6 Paul Ricoeur, *The Rule of Metaphor: Multi-Disciplinary Studies of the Creation of Meaning in Language* (University of Toronto Press, 1977).

7 Wikipedia, 'Surfside Condominium Collapse', https://en.wikipedia.org/wiki/Surfside_condominium_collapse.

8 This is the very first point made by Immanuel Kant in establishing experience as the ground of all understanding, in *Critique of Pure Reason*, trans. P. Guyer and A. W. Wood (Cambridge University Press, 1998), A2.

9 Paul Hawken, *Blessed Unrest: How the Largest Movement in the World Came into Being, and Why No One Saw It Coming* (Viking Press, 2007).

10 See http://www.leading-causes.com.

11 William R. Burch et al., *The Structure and Dynamics of Human Ecosystems: Toward a Model for Understanding and Action* (Yale University Press, 2017).

Chapter 2

CAPACITIES

Hoe, plough, waterwheel, windmill; thread, loom, paper, printing press;
cabin, skyscraper, bridge; ship, rocket, Mars-lander;
clock, radio, TV; abacus, computer, cellphone;
syringe, pacemaker, CAT-scanner.

Axe, bow & arrow, blunderbuss, rifle, flame-thrower; landmine, torpedo;
helicopter, bomber, missiles, drone; thumbscrews, rack, iron-maiden;
guillotine, electric chair; Auschwitz, H-bomb, agent orange.

Play, cook, teach, preach, caress, shame, forgive, sing.

Harmonica, marimba, sitar; flute, trumpet; piano, organ, orchestra.

Code, regulation, decree, creed, covenant, contract;
parliament, judiciary, constitution.

We begin with a basic point about what it means to be human. As the above
lists make clear, we make and do things again and again, in countless ways.
Each item listed is human-made, not found, each born of a particular kind
of human activity. The first two lists are opposed, one constructive, the other
destructive. The third is not about objects; the fourth about capturing sound
and feel. The last is social. Tens of thousands of names for millions of creative
acts which humans do as naturally as breathing. How do they happen? What
have they to do with being deeply accountable for the life we live? An iconic
story sets us on the way.

'What Hath God Wrought?'

In 1844 this somewhat archaically formulated question, a quotation from
Numbers in the Hebrew Bible, was the first message ever sent, from Samuel
Morse and Alfred Vail, by telegraph, the early predecessor of the Internet and
email. They used what we have known ever since as Morse code. It was sent

at the completion of the first transmission line between Washington DC and Baltimore and travelled just forty miles.

God did not do any of this, though one might claim that God made the creature who possesses the capacities necessary to make the instrument, build the transmission line, compose the message and devise the code. *Capacity* is the crucial word; it signals an inherent human faculty that can be applied in many ways, and the more we understand its creative power, the more confidence and courage we will have to move boldly as we must.

Human capacities include the ability to see deeply into nature (e.g. identifying the force of electricity, an invisible energy), to imagine a possibility otherwise not present in nature (a machine and cables to harness this energy) using symbolic systems we invent (language, Morse code, mathematics and more), thereby giving us the ability to transform nature in ways otherwise impossible.

The lists at the top of this chapter represent a quite extraordinary range of creative activities yet still only hint at all we have made or done in the world. They are almost never the result of just one isolated person, for we express our capacities through the relationships and systems that themselves are made, unmade, done and undone, brought into being and stabilized with intention. Nothing is more fundamental to being human, and we may rightfully call this our 'creative freedom'. It is *creative* because what we make is new and otherwise not present in nature; it is *freedom* because we experience ourselves as being able to act in ways not wholly determined – even if always constrained – by nature. Thus, we alter nature and ourselves.[1]

This has at least two implications for being deeply accountable. The first is that it removes the idea that we are passive recipients of events external to us, emphasizing the fact that we are actively and intentionally *causal agents* in the world. This is true *to a degree* that is decisive beyond any other sentient or intelligent creature of which we know. No matter how cute a dog or cat is, it cannot do this and is thus not accountable in the same way as we are. The effects of the astonishing range of complexity and potency of this activity ripple out through time and across space, down through generations and into the future. Most importantly, what we do, we can undo.

The second implication is that this capacity to make and unmake, to do or undo, lies in irrevocable ambiguity: it can aim at life or at death. The *use* we make of our creative freedom, the ends to which we direct it, can be as destructive as it can be creative.

Intentionality Matters

Some may question whether we really do have this much freedom.[2] To be sure, there are clear limits on our freedom. First, we cannot avoid or wholly overcome the external, heteronomous effects of the relations, institutions and systems that shape and contain us, but without which we would not be human. Second, we do not easily control or comprehend the potent emotional and psychological forces at work in us that appear to us as a contradiction to our will (Paul, in Romans 7:15–20, recognizes this, but attributes it to 'sin').

Third, much as we might like to, we cannot predict the results of even our best-intended choices; we simply do not control the consequences of our actions. We can and should *consider* those consequences, but that's not the same as controlling them. Recognizing this implies constant humility in the face of unintended consequences. They will always scatter unpredictably beyond our limits. Like unforced errors that even at the highest tennis levels decide one-third of the points, no matter how wise or experienced we believe ourselves to be, things often turn out quite differently than we could possibly foresee.

Nonetheless, we are *not* wholly determined either by external forces and circumstances, by biological functions and dysfunctions or by the internal drives and desires of the psyche. Those factors play a role, sometimes quite powerfully, in how and why we act. We instinctively take to flight or fight when faced with a threat; we experience depression and apathy when significant hormonal or chemical imbalances occur in our system; we act out when we are humiliated or rejected, as any human knows. Still, unless we are so crushed or broken as no longer to respond beyond our impulses and instincts, nothing takes away our capacity to decide to what ends we shall live and how.

Put differently, nothing annuls our intrinsic humanity, as people who have confronted the direst circumstances have repeatedly demonstrated. We may not be able to control the consequences of our actions, but, however influenced by others past and present (always the case to varying degrees), *we*, and not someone else, decide what we *intend* and why. In this very special and important sense, we are fully responsible for our actions and for whether we intend generative or destructive ends, good or evil, mere self-interest or the interest of all. This (not individualism) is the true meaning of autonomy. No small thing, it makes accountability real.

In sum, in drawing on the capacities of creative freedom we possess to act with causal effect in the world, in the process transforming both nature and ourselves, we are responsible for our intentions, that is, for the subjective grounds upon which we orient ourselves towards others in the world. In this very precise sense we are, independently of any consequences, *morally responsible* for what we intend with the use of our creative freedom.

This is so central to deep accountability that it needs to be unpacked a bit further.

The Moral of the Story

Consider the name we give to our kind of creature: *Homo sapiens sapiens*. The standard taxonomic label for the modern human being, it's nice to think that it means we are a twice times 'wise' or 'discerning' (*sapiens*) creature of the genus *Homo*. Yet, in truth, adding a second *sapiens* really signifies nothing special, only that we are a subspecies of *Homo sapiens*. Moreover, we know that at least one other subspecies, *neanderthalensis*, also made tools, controlled fire, had some cultural creativity including social structures, and gave us a bit of its DNA. Still, perhaps that double *sapiens* suggests something particularly astute or discerning about the modern human being, about us, about our creative freedom, which is a source of both hope and accountability.

There are two common criticisms of our perspective. One, as we have noted, is that we overstate the distinctiveness of the creative capacities of human beings. Another, somewhat contradictory, is that we insufficiently acknowledge how dangerous human beings are. With regard to the latter, we don't at all doubt the misplaced use of our capacities that produce the well-documented failures and 'sins' of our species. Yet we consider our basic point to be face valid: We *do* have a causal impact in the world and, to the extent that we *intend* what we do (whether by commission or omission), we are directly responsible or accountable for it no matter what else may apply. To suggest otherwise releases all accountability and leads to hell on earth.

Are humans really that distinctive, however? Isn't the claim that we are decisively distinctive making the same mistake of assuming a superiority that has brought such harm and suffering to other creatures and nature itself? Aren't we being far too anthropocentric about our capacities, ignoring that other species beside *Homo sapiens* have consciousness or intelligence of some kind or another, including birds and insects?[3] Bees, for example, demonstrate a surprising complexity of behaviour that should undermine any idea of our self-importance in the schemes of nature.

It is surely right and good to question our uniqueness as human beings. We should not forget that we are creatures of nature, bound to nature in ways that are vital to our own thriving, down to the cellular level,[4] owing our existence to the whole. We are in trouble if we think we are set apart from every other creature in ways that authorize us to do with them as we wish and damn the consequences. Inappropriately confident of the powers of our mind and the technologies we are capable of inventing, we then become destructive of the very source of our shared earthly household, our *oikos*. We risk destroying the whole, ourselves included.

For such reasons, some would say that instead of focusing on human uniqueness, we should pay more humble attention to the ecology of which we are part and which we share with such an amazing variety of forms of life. We would be wiser to recognize that our minds are bodied – not just *embodied* as if something still implicitly separate – and that, as body-mind, we are the same as other creatures of intelligence, indeed, with all of organic life. We agree.

Nonetheless, this should not detract us from the deep accountability we bear for our very distinctive capacities. No matter how much we regard ourselves as one with nature, as merely another kind of creature among many with no special rights over others and no authority to damage or destroy their lives or worlds, we remain uniquely potent in our ability, through the capacities of spirit we possess, to affect them in ways that are otherwise unprecedented, and to do so knowingly. This point is also made by Hans Jonas, whose philosophy has since become a core element of global environmental justice movements. Already some forty years ago, in the preface to the English edition of his book, *The Imperative of Responsibility*, he wrote:

> Modern technology, informed by an ever-deeper penetration of nature and propelled by the forces of market and politics, has enhanced human power beyond anything known or even dreamed of before. It is a power of a matter, of a life on earth, and over man himself [*sic*]; and it keeps growing at an accelerating pace.[5]

His book is a comprehensive call to recognize that 'responsibility is a correlate of power and must be commensurate with the latter's scope and that of its exercise'.[6] This is particularly clear when we notice that we do in fact hold each other as human beings accountable for our intentions in ways that we would not even begin to expect of other creatures. We expect that even a very young child learns that they cannot do whatever they wish without consequences. We do not expect a dog, a dolphin, an octopus or a chimpanzee to meet the same standards at all. Nor do we see them or any other creature putting in place sophisticated institutions, codes of conduct, courts and other means of regulating conduct that require reasonable grounds for what they do, failing which some kind of punishment or sanction would be applied.

Sapiens sapiens – wise about being wise, or, put differently, capable of self-reflection and judgement in ways that exceed anything else of which we know. Accountable both for our place in the world and for what we intend and do in it.

Burden and Gift

Let us then not seek any veil of innocence covered by the pretence that we are mere creatures of nature distinguished only by high levels of skill. We are also, fundamentally, creatures of will, who must decide how to live, for whom and for what ends. Our extraordinary capacities are then not a sign of superiority; they are a sign of responsibility. This is a burden we dare not lighten or ignore. It is also a gift, the pearl of joy found only when our intentions are aligned with what matters most for the life of the whole.

In what sense is it a gift? Quite simply, we did not give ourselves those capacities. However they came into being – through divine act or a long process of evolution and neurological development – they are *a priori*, that is, intrinsic to what it means to be human and, thus, as long as we remain human, inalienable. As a gift, our supersensible capacities for creative freedom deserve to be treated with respect and with humility.

The gift is also a burden, for it requires that we act accordingly, intentionally, aware of the radical ambiguity of the powers of our freedom that enable us to destroy as much as to create. Because we are genuinely free, both good and evil are possible for us as a matter of choice about what governs our intentions and our actions. If this were not so, if every intention and every action would be determined by some external factor – our genes, our upbringing, our psychological drives, our culture, our environment and so on – then we would be accountable for nothing, and no one should hold us to account.

There is a second gift to acknowledge: the world itself. We may make many things, but we did not make the world. We are given the world we live in. Both the world and nature are, in this sense, gifts. Whatever we do with the capacities we possess, themselves a gift, to nature and the world either honours or dishonours, respects or disrespects the very basis of our existence and of life itself. What we have done over the last handful of centuries has begun to alter our environment to such an extent that it no longer conforms to its long-established rhythms and now threatens to blow back at us. It may be much slower than the impact of the asteroid that might have killed off the dinosaurs, but it may well be roughly equivalent in effect.

Yet we are not totally helpless in this regard. We are not powerless to change the future any less than other humans changed the past. This is not just a matter of skill, as important as that will be in terms of new technologies and a better understanding of nature and its limits. It is also a matter of will which, right now, is deeply challenged by the scale and pace of the situation we face.

Beyond Self-Interest

What we intend with the use of our human capacities really is a matter of will. It is an expression of the creative freedom we possess over and above anything or anyone that may otherwise constrain or determine us. Free in this sense, we are entirely capable of making decisions that reflect our mere self-interest – or that of people, societies, nations or other kinds of groups to which we belong – whatever the effects on others. Some kinds of self-interest surely have their place (food, safety, affirmation, to be treated justly and so on) and, indeed, there is at least one view that attracts many, that of Ayn Rand, which treats the maximization of self-interest as rational and the highest virtue.[7]

Clearly this is not our view. We take the side of those who recognize that our creative freedom makes us equally as capable of intentionally seeking arrangements and solutions that go beyond self-interest for the sake of all and for the sake of the whole, even perhaps against one's self-interest (with potential costs that must be accepted). This is what we mean by deep accountability. Whenever and wherever we see it in action in the life of a particular person or group of people, we recognize it and honour it, aware that it calls something forth from us too of which we are capable and through which we find deep meaning and an affirmation of life.

We link this here to what our human capacities make possible. We acknowledge, too, that many think that's not all there is or all that is going on, that another creative force is involved, that the gift of our capacities with their possibilities yet emerging and of the world we did not make comes from One who created it all.

Whatever your view, deep accountability is not a burden that weighs down on life and dulls it. It is not born in isolation. The living of it happens within webs of relationships that are not merely for the labour and the lift. Those we think with and work with are not beasts of burden, but creatures of joy that emerge when the right things are done well for those we love. The intelligence of work done together with joy gives us the energy and power we need. To joy we now turn.

Notes

1 For a full exposition of these points and their implications, see Douglas R. McGaughey and James R. Cochrane, *The Human Spirit: Groundwork* (SUN Press, 2017).

2 Jonathan Haidt, for example, in *The Righteous Mind: Why Good People Are Divided by Politics and Religion* (Vintage Books, 2013), has proposed that our belief about our freedom is largely a fabrication, suggesting that we, driven by internal forces and external pressures, have far less control than we imagine. In his metaphor, we are more like a rider on an elephant who is under the illusion that he is steering it when it largely goes its own way.

3 See New York University, 'The New York Declaration on Animal Consciousness', 19 April 2024, https://sites.google.com/nyu.edu/nydeclaration/declaration.

4 See David Quammen, *The Tangled Tree: A Radical New History of Life* (Simon & Schuster, 2018).

5 Hans Jonas, *The Imperative of Responsibility: In Search of an Ethics for the Technological Age* (University of Chicago Press, 1985), ix; original German edition: *Das Prinzip Verantwortung: Versuch Einer Ethik Für die Technologische Zivilisation (*Suhrkamp Verlag, 1979).
6 Jonas, *The Imperative of Responsibility*, x.
7 See https://en.wikipedia.org/wiki/Rational_egoism.

Chapter 3

JOY

The world has enough books on problems and problem-solving. But we will solve little if we do not turn first in the direction of joy. We are referring here not merely to an emotion but to something that resonates in every cell and synapse of our lives, especially when aligned with whom and where, we find sustaining life in what matters most. There is an intelligence, a deep knowing, we may call joy. Joy is not what we experience as an end. Joy is how we navigate, the evidence that we are on the right track, doing the right work with the right people in the right way. When in doubt, move boldly towards joy.

This may seem an incongruous provocation. We are so accustomed to the bombardment of the negative that speaking of joy might seem tone-deaf. Can one really talk about 'joy' if one is at the receiving end of the death-dealing dynamics of poverty, unemployment, war or grievous personal loss? Is this not simply inappropriate? Without a doubt, it isn't always the right place, time or moment to speak of joy. A beloved person suddenly facing the news of terminal cancer, a parent who has just lost a child in aching agony, an unrequitable anger about death and destruction in one's home occasioned by war or terror – these are not occasions to call for joy. As Ecclesiastes has it, wisdom is recognizing that there is a time for everything, and not every time is right for joy.

Still, over time, there is no capacity for human creativity or agency without the flow of joy. This is why it is crucial in a book about deep accountability that we begin here. It is not fear, but joy, that will guide you towards the deep accountability we are made for. The threats, the hurts, the challenges, the uncertainties could make one pretty depressed and disheartened. Precisely then, it's easy to forget the radical importance of joy.

Perhaps a story from Horst, one of our 'Leading Causes of Life Fellows', helps. He remembers a particularly dark time in his life. Considered a threat to the South African Apartheid state in the early 1970s, he was detained without trial and isolated in prison. He had no access to lawyers, books or other people than his warders. And he waited to be interrogated by a dreaded man whose nickname was Spyker ('the nail'), acquired by virtue of a torture technique for which he was known. Uncertain if even his whiteness would protect him, life became suspended for Horst. Everything around him was dark grey, from the bars on the cell to his darkening and diminishing spirit. This is as far as one can be from joy.

One day, across the hall, Horst noticed a cat, which seemed to notice him too. With a feline sway, it walked slowly towards him. Eventually, it brushed up against the bars. Too close to put his whole hand through, he extended his fingers to touch the fur. The cat moved with what Horst could only feel as a gentle caring for the nearly lost human being. Decades later, Horst still speaks of the strange feeling when his chin began an almost forgotten movement: he smiled. Rediscovering his ability to smile was for him the epitome of joy. It healed his wounded spirit and helped him survive.

This is ground to be walked on only with great sensitivity and care. Yet joy may be among the most important things to talk about – as one radical root to our strength and, at the same time, the North Star by which we can dependably navigate. Otherwise, while we may breathe, we may not live.

No Use Without Joy

Another story, a personal one, adds to the picture. Many years ago, I (Jim), much younger then, was selected as part of a five-person delegation from South Africa, sponsored by the World Council of Churches, for a three-month study tour of youth work in Palestine/Israel and parts of Europe, including the United Kingdom. Back home I was active in the Cape Office of the Christian Institute of Southern Africa (CI), an overtly anti-Apartheid group led by the high-profile Afrikaner, Beyers Naudé.[1] These were particularly rough years, the time of Horst's incarceration. The government functioned as a police state, with solid blessing from the largest Afrikaner Dutch Reformed Church (DRC), to which most of the cabinet ministers in government belonged.

At the time of the Sharpeville Massacre in 1961, Naudé was the DRC's second most senior cleric, but he now concluded that Apartheid was a heresy that could not be supported by his faith. Branded a traitor by his own community and the government, he was forced to resign from his church. Refusing to accept his fate or go quietly, he founded the CI. It was a serious stab at the ideological heart of the Apartheid state and its official policy, known as Christian Nationalism.[2] As time went on, the CI and its people increasingly came under surveillance from the Special Branch, the security police. It was also attacked by right-wing Whites in collusion with the police. In Cape Town, shots were fired into living rooms (no one was killed, fortunately), and arsonists set fire to places where the CI met. Many of those with whom the CI was in solidarity, including some of its own members, were detained without trial, some dying under torture. Others fell to their death 'by mistake' out of a police office window or died 'slipping on a bar of soap' in the shower.

It was during the early part of these dark years that I went on the WCC study tour. When we arrived in Geneva, we stayed as guests of the WCC in John Knox House. Here, we were asked to speak of ourselves. I shared some of my history with the Christian Institute. Afterwards, a tall, imposing young Black man from Guinea came over. Calm and composed but utterly serious, he expressed appreciation of what I had shared but, looking frankly into my eyes, said he needed to say something else. He was personally connected to the exiled South African liberation movement, and he wanted me to be clear about something. No matter how much I might side with the Black struggle, he said, or 'betrayed' what Whites regard as their own interests, I willy-nilly remained one of the oppressor-group. A clear and identifiable beneficiary, there was, as he puts it, 'a bullet with my name on it'. I needed to know this and understand what it meant.

I did; and not superficially. Instantly, it changed the way I saw everything. I was already well aware of the possible personal consequences of a commitment to the CI and the anti-Apartheid struggle, even if my whiteness lent me some protection. Still, this was an existential moment of choice. If, in the mind of those fighting for their liberation, I was already dead, then I might as well live *as if I am dead*. That was a surprisingly freeing thought, to live each day as if it's my last. Why waste time or energy on hoarding life? Just do what is right.

There was more. During a traumatized night I struggled with another existential question: If I don't *actually* die, could I still celebrate life in the midst of the struggle to do the right thing? Could I, once back in South Africa, even dare to enjoy a meal, watch the sun sink over the sea or relax into the beauty of the classical music I was learning to appreciate? Was everything entirely a struggle for justice without remainder? Would my complicity in the oppression of others through my relatively privileged and safe life make any enjoyment and celebration poisoned fruit? Did my humanity, my soul, dissolve in the relentless grind of an all-consuming cause?

For help, I turned to the head of the Youth Department at the WCC, Albert van den Heuvel, an inspiration to many of us. He knew my situation in South Africa well, personally knew many of my compatriots and mentors, understood why I was asking and listened with patience and compassion. What he said still resonates, releasing the light within: 'Jim, On the day you can no longer celebrate anything, on the day that there is *no* joy left in your life, that's the day you must leave South Africa. Then you are of no use to anyone, least of all yourself.'

Joy as Resistance

Clearly, not everyone can escape their situation, and that's not trivial. But equally clearly, a vital energy, sustaining oneself and others around one, is missing when one can no longer laugh in the face of threats, or joke about those who think they control one's life or place, or find joy in vital companionship even in desperate situations, more profound than what one experiences in normal safety and happiness. Radical joy taps deep.

Few have expressed this better than Elie Wiesel in *The Gates of the Forest*, the post-Holocaust story – only semi-fictional[3] – of Gregor, a boy escaping Germany, finding various hiding places as he journeys, but who wants to know in the face of the terror 'where God is hiding'. Along the way, he repeatedly hears his companion Gavriel's laughter, which appears thoroughly absurd. But it is not:

> You mustn't forget laughter either. Do you know what laughter is? It's God's mistake. When God made man in order to bend him to his wishes, he carelessly gave him the gift of laughter. Little did he know that later that earthworm would use it as a weapon of vengeance. When he found out, there was nothing he could do; it was too late to take back the gift. And yet he tried his best. He drove man out of paradise, invented an infinite variety of sins and punishments, and made him conscious of his own nothingness, all in order to prevent him from laughing. But, as I say, it was too late. God made a mistake before man made his. What they have in common is that they are both irreparable.[4]

This is laughter as resistance, as a reaction against the absurd, as an act of rebellion. In Juliana Claassens's formulation, it is a 'creative, extra-linguistic' response to suffering in the face of the rupture of language by which to comprehend atrocity; it is an 'interruption of the system and the state of oppression'.[5] More than this (citing Jacqueline Busie in *The Laughter of the Oppressed*): 'The laughter of the oppressed testifies to the existence of an autonomous self who not only exists but also makes choices independent of social authorities and thinks outside their ideological framework.' It is 'a means of maintaining one's subjectivity and dignity in the midst of dignity-denying circumstances'.

Most of the above is about tragic laughter, laughter in the face of severe trauma; it's not about joy or celebration. Yet a key element is already in Busie's articulation: the existence of an autonomous self who makes choices about how they want to live and act independent of heteronomous authorities and ideologies (including religious frameworks). Here we need to be very careful. Autonomy here is not about being free of others (individualism) or choosing between alternatives (exchange relations). Rather, it is what the word actually means: 'giving yourself the law', that is, intentionally deciding how and why you act and live in the world at any moment whatever other influences on you there might be (and there are many, of course). As we've said already, that capacity is inherent; it cannot be taken away from us other than by death. It is what oppression cannot kill unless it kills the body or destroys the mind. So we laugh at those who think they have power they do not.

This capacity, precisely this capacity, is also the source of joy. That's the key point of Albert van den Heuvel's caution. It's a key aspect of the iconic story of Job as he wrangles with his friends about the disasters he has faced and ultimately accuses God. There is no real resolution at the end but, rather, 'an act of protest itself, as an attempt to embrace the fragility and the goodness of life', one that articulates 'the incongruities of existence in which celebration and festivity occur side-by-side with evil and death'.[6]

The Radical Nature of Joy

Joy – celebration and festivity – is radical because it springs from what is possible for us, for everyone, despite trauma and evil, in the midst of trauma and evil. It's not frivolity, escapism, thoughtlessness, insensitivity or foolishness. It's a spring of vitality, a flow of energy, a spirit that refuses death and celebrates life. In the words of a beloved professor, Ross Snyder,

> We celebrate, not ourselves, but the forces which make the human. [...] taking into one's consciousness, the full range of the human condition, and in such a way as to sense the human dignity present. [...] Celebrative existence is expressive, rather than reactive. Our imagination stirs, a wild exuberance begins to flow. It takes on form, pattern, structure, relationship. Now undivided energies pour into the shaping of the world of meaning. The invisible within us becomes visible. Celebration is a mode of relationship. It is not a spectacle, viewed by people who remain impervious to each other.[7]

One needs to imagine joy to survive. And joy is often present in the inspired moment when the creative image becomes clear, when curiosity is met by excitement and pleasure. We laugh out loud as the sea parts, the perfect solution drops in place, the missing part is found, when we say yes to love. It is less obvious that joy is necessary in the more mundane labours of life.

Think of the most astonishing movement of the honeybee hive as one hive becomes two. At first, one hardly notices, but in minutes the sky surrounding the hive is filled with bees flying hard and wild in widening 50-foot circles and just as high above the ground. The air is alive with exuberant frenzy.

After minutes of seeming chaos, some of the bees begin to cluster on a nearby tree limb, gradually forming a nearly solid mass the size of a soccer ball. Others still whirl, but even amid the riot, some of the older bees are already alight with purpose, seeking the place known deep in their DNA that will be the next permanent hive.

That decision will determine if the new hive offers the conditions in which it can survive the next winter or not: a big enough cavity, dry, high and defensible. The swarm considers the options brought back by the scouts and communicated by an intricate dance, weighing the choices on the basis of the enthusiasm of the dancers. Then, inspired and informed, the hive flies with its queen to the new home it could not have anticipated back in the safety of the old dark box where they had all been born and raised for this very moment. The next hive finds its way in joy, guided by dance through many risks and lives to taste the nectar of a thousand springtime blooms. Which is the joy, which the work and what the fruit? Every step is, every one of them.

Joy is neither a precursor to nor the inspiration for agency. Henri Nouwen calls it the fruit of compassion.[8] In other words, it is an effect, a quality that emerges like the forgotten capacity to smile as one finds that one is acknowledged, still an actor and not just an observer, in the drama of life. Nor is joy merely personal. Whether acting in response to climate change, radical inequality or any other challenge of our time, there is an inexpressible social dynamic to this kind of joy that wells up from within unsought, enabling oneself and others to move into the space between those also moved to act.

Confronted with the abyss, one needs to see a way out of the hurt, trauma or rage one is feeling or experiencing. Joy will not simply arrive, especially without some kind of meaningful connection, even with something as apparently trivial as the cat in Horst's cell. Those of us who can have a responsibility to facilitate or evoke it to become what we may call 'theogenerative practitioners'.[9]

This happens in many ways. Singing freedom songs in the era at the darkest time of Apartheid South Africa was a source of joy. A ritual celebration of lament may help one break free from depression and begin to taste joy again. A coherent story with a hopeful narrative may be a condition for joy. It could be as simple as one told to us by Beulah, one of our LCLI Fellows, about her mother who, after dressing in the morning, goes out actively *anticipating* that something will happen that brings joy, whether in the bus she rides or on the streets where she walks, with the unsurprising consequence that she regularly brings joy to others in the process. In so choosing, she expresses her agency, another condition for joy to emerge. Similarly, in Cape Town, in communities stressed and constrained under Covid-19 conditions and short of resources, people established Community Action Networks to take into their own hands the agency that had been taken away from them and find a coherent response to the challenges.

Some critical questions arise at this point. Does joy have any purchase at a larger scale? What does it mean to speak of joy at an institutional or community level or at a social scale? Would that force us to change our concept of agency, given that have little control of much beyond our immediate spheres of influence or activity? Is it not important to recognize *degrees* of suffering or joy, and do we need to tease out the relationship between pain, suffering and joy as a triumvirate?

Leaving these questions still open, we are reminded that Darwin implied that life moves forward through competition, even violence, death and starvation. Spencer gave him the language we know: 'survival of the fittest'. This is surely an inadequate explanation of how life works. And this dangerous oversimplification amplifies our fear-mongering and makes us overlook some of our greatest capacities for creative adaptation in our radical times. We have often turned, instead, towards Jonas Salk, brought to life in our dialogues by his colleague Heather Wood Ion, another LCLI Fellow, who teaches us how central joy was as a diagnostic tool with those who came to him for guidance about questions great, small, profound and strategic. Expecting prescriptions from him, he typically asked questions about where they found joy, and about what that might signal about where they would find life and work worthy of their hopes. 'What makes your heart leap?' is a far more useful strategic question than 'what are you most worried about?' It brings to view *dunamis* – the power already moving in one's life.

This is, of course, deeply inspiring. But to call it inspiring is to miss the point that one of the great scientists of our era used joy with almost surgical precision to make evident and actionable the heartbeat in the phenomenon, whether that living instance is one life of a patient or a social initiative or, in some cases, a planetary project. Fear grows from the past and focuses on what might cease, what might hurt. It narrows the focus while joy opens the mind and heart, then gives reason a harness worthy of life. Joy is about what is next. Move boldly towards joy.

Notes

1 Peter Walshe, *Church Versus State in South Africa: The Case of the Christian Institute* (C. Hurst, and Orbis Books, 1983).

2 That history should be a warning to all who trade in the currency of Christian nationalism.

3 Elie Wiesel and his family ended up in Auschwitz where he and his father were used as labour (his mother and sister were murdered). The two of them were later transferred to Buchenwald which he, but not his father, survived. Wiesel campaigned for

the rights of minorities or oppressed communities elsewhere, including South Africa, but – an extraordinary if explainable blind spot – not for Palestinians, even supporting the extension of Jewish settlements into Palestinian areas, a fundamental contradiction given his passion otherwise for human dignity and rights.

4 Elie Wiesel, *The Gates of the Forest* (Holt, Reinhardt and Winston, 1966), 21.
5 Claassens, L. Juliana, 'Tragic Laughter: Laughter as Resistance in the Book of Job', *Interpretation: A Journal of Bible and Theology* 69, no. 2 (2015): 143–55.
6 Ibid., 154 (citing Whedbee in the second quote).
7 Ross Snyder, *Contemporary Celebration* (Abingdon Press, 1971), 32–3, 45.
8 Henri Nouwen, *Here and Now: Living in the Spirit* (Crossroad Publishing, 1994), 37ff.
9 Gary's neologism; see Gary Gunderson, 'Theogenerative Life and Practice,' in *Handbook on Religion and Health: Pathways for a Turbulent World*, ed. James R. Cochrane et al. (Edward Elgar, 2024), 97–112.

Chapter 4

STORM

I can tell by the way the trees beat, after
so many dull days, on my worried windowpanes
that a storm is coming,
and I hear the far-off fields say things
I cannot bear without a friend,
cannot love without a sister.
Rainer Maria Rilke[1]

The storm is upon us now, not far off. And the reasons are entirely predictable; no mystery is involved at all. The structure of our modern way of life is like a sharp stick poking the planetary beast, ensuring the storm you and I are experiencing and should have expected. While we humans see the storm as a break *down*, planetary complexity is more of a *breakthrough* from nature's perspective. It's not just nature; it's also the stuff of egregious, systemic distortions of the social fabric that drive anger, resentment, alienation and popular mobilization. Again, we should have expected what we are now experiencing. The phenomenon leading from undeserved privilege to humiliation is the stuff of myth. The Greeks called that painfully relevant myth Nemesis.

Nemesis is the goddess that wreaks justice on the proud who are always shocked that their power of which they were proud did not make them invulnerable. The privileged are likewise surprised to find that their privileges are temporary. Nemesis comes not just for the obvious drivers of injustice but also for those of us who may simply be floating along with the tide of privilege. Nemesis focuses on any privilege that is undeserved, especially if it uses up a future opportunity of someone else. Nemesis is the highly inconvenient god for us.

She has been coming for some time. The lacing anger of Greta Thunberg and many others, a full half-century after the Club of Rome's report on *The Limits to Growth*,[2] about a generational dereliction of duty around climate change action, not only points to the failure of those of us old enough to know better, but it also drives home the doubts about whether the rich and powerful

– and those of us who benefit from the world they have made – will do the right thing at all. It falls, too, on any of us who, through quiet acquiescence, act to support systems we did not invent but from which we benefit at the cost of others.

The only surprise of Nemesis is that it creates a storm that batters not only the rich and powerful who would seem to deserve it. It also rains on those of us who may feel alienated from meaningful decisions about our lives, even resentful of elites, experts and the hubris they represent. Why should it rain on us, too? Ask anyone on the Gulf Coast; a hurricane is not a precision weapon. Ask anyone in the mountains far from the sea, where its wind and rain eliminate entire towns filled with environmentalists.

These are large and complex phenomena. In the Midwest of the United States, this kind of storm can be hundreds of miles across, with many tor-nado-bearing storm cells involved, each capable of levelling entire towns. Rilke's metaphorical storm has spun off many into institutional tornadoes that scramble the lines between entire sectors of the economy. But nowhere is the storm more painfully and ironically felt than in the domain of healthcare, with its complex web of privileged institutions on which we depend at our most vulnerable moments.

Medical Nemesis

Among the most inconvenient books of the twentieth century for those in the fields of applied health sciences was *Medical Nemesis*, written by Ivan Illich and published in 1975.[3] Nearly unreadably dense and easy to dismiss for its savagely confrontational prose, a half-century later Illich's core insight is only harder to avoid: 'The medical establishment has become a major threat to health.' Long before the lamentable response to the two viral pandemics of our era, HIV/AIDS and Covid-19, and long before the triumphs in treatment (though not over) for diabetes and other diseases of the metabolic syndrome, Illich saw that the most highly privileged and richly funded professions of our time, brilliant as they are, failed to fulfil their most basic promise – that of increasing the likelihood of improved health and well-being for most of the population.

One could (and we will) make the same observation about other modern patterns of privilege that we were also counting on to protect the natural sys-tems on which life depends. We will all need a medical professional, probably a hospital, some day. We breathe air and drink water, too.

Before we dive into Illich's insights into the medical storm, it is crucial to keep in mind that his inconvenient clarity about health applies more broadly. He saw how systems with self-reinforcing and accelerating patterns of privileges unfairly absorb resources, finance and talent away from other parts of society.[4] At the same time, Nemesis also hurts those *inside* the systems who appear to benefit unfairly. They are sometimes surprised to find their own life, spirit, time and talent also sucked away into the service of a system they did not intend to serve. So too with institutions of finance, education, religion and agriculture.

It has long been true that hospitals, while not a bad thing in themselves, are dangerous for those who are patients due to the high complexity of the procedures. Perfection is impossible and mistakes are inevitable; thus, any unnecessary day inside the hospital is an unnecessary risk. It is also dangerous in a different way for those who work there, with the least privileged employees in the most direct exposure to risk.

Due to the density of the environment, transmission of infectious disease is a constant risk even in the very best of circumstances, much less amid pandemics or when political vitriol makes adherence to viral protocols uneven. The emotionally fraught nature of intensive care amid unrealistic expectations of miracles makes conflict and even violence a common reality.

Any modern hospital demands a massive investment of human and material resources, all managed by administrators entirely shaped by hospital logic. The machinery creates a financial cyclone rising like a hurricane from the circulation of vast expenditure, highly paid professionals and structured revenue flowing from public and private payers. The financial phenomenon of modern healthcare is arguably justified by the suffering and the promise of healing, but it often draws energy and money from the life of the wider community.

If all this was absolutely essential to the healing, it might be accepted. Illich's insight cuts exactly to the core here, at the foundational logic. He sees that not all of the complexity is driven by science; much simply extrapolates institutional inertia while ignoring the growing body of knowledge of the science of prevention and the role of social dynamics that should make high-tech intervention less necessary. Even while institutional healthcare draws money aggressively towards hospitals, science actually points out the door into the social dynamics of the neighbourhoods. Institutional healthcare claims a privilege that is not necessary for the healing, and where this is not justified, it is unjust. Nemesis will come.

Contradictions pile up on each other like a gathering storm. As Illich observed, those in positions of influence and apparent control of these systems struggle to change or challenge the systemic dynamics. As they are themselves produced by and serve the system that employs them, it is hard for them to see alternatives to the standard thinking about how to deploy and value the assets of the system. The system serves itself; it has a logical imperative of its own, different from the logic of those it is supposed to serve. System imperatives are gnostic when it comes to the lifeworlds of persons,[5] operating independently of the human agents whose primary purpose is to serve particular roles and tasks steered by the strategic, instrumental goals of the system.

Many of the most important decisions in healthcare are not made by scientists but by the high priests of modern healthcare – the financial acolytes, who are usually not physicians. The finance people tend to have impeccable personal values, but they have not been shaped by the broader health sciences. Those managing the financial apparatus of healthcare thus live within the sharp limitations of their intellectual formation. Even medical practitioners in senior management tend to be schooled in interventional biomedicine, rarely immersed in public health prevention science or the social sciences. The pattern of resulting decisions is almost predictable, as are the deadly results of the misalignment between the centripetal vision of health science and the gravitational demands of institutional reality.

Illich pays no attention to the damage this does to those who work in, lead, manage and build strategy as professionals in a healthcare and public health organization. They feel Nemesis in their bones as a sense of surprising betrayal. Lives of privilege that fail to satisfy; lives of power that fail to fulfil. From top to bottom, these webs of privilege fail to provide the joy or fulfilment one might expect of lives spent in institutions focused on healing and well-being.

Altruistic Nemesis

Nemesis may take special aim at institutions that claim to be altruistic and then fail to fulfil their mission. All of the contradictions of healthcare organizations are, oddly, more problematic within those legally defined in the United States of America as 'not-for-profit', most of them established by religious groups. One can hardly blame purely corporate healthcare for focusing on the science around which a profitable business is built; it has no need to pretend otherwise. But non-profit healthcare organizations tend to ask *fewer* basic questions about how money bends the imagination towards which ends, precisely because it is assumed that any institutional growth is good for its stated mission. Their leaders believe their own brochures and are often less, not more, thoughtful about which science they bend to its service. Few hospitals know about public health science or use any of it to determine their capital commitments. Hence the storm, hence Nemesis.

Having served in senior management of two non-profit healthcare systems, both regarded as exemplars of community benefit within the broader field, Gary has watched Boards of Directors approve the commitment of a half billion dollars for a new surgical tower block without ever weighing that multi-decade commitment against the actual mission of the organization. These hospitals were founded by religious people who intended to improve the health of the local community by harnessing health science in partnership with government policy and the community networks of goodwill. As they have grown in scale, beyond the imagination of the founders, what began as a partnership has been increasingly defined and governed by a logic built on finance that plays by entirely different rules and ethics. Nemesis would say this is utterly unsurprising – but not inevitable. Systems, after all, are established by us and, despite their power, they are not beyond the judgement of the god of fairness.

What exactly do financial logic, or its logicians, miss along the way? Those trained to measure transactions, exchanges, the costs of things (and costs of money itself) easily and somewhat accidentally guide their organizations to serve their own ends instead of those of their founders. The financial mind overestimates its ability to comprehend the cascading complexity of the transactions it tracks. That's because human beings frequently act in ways not amenable to calculation and formulaic assessment.

Financial acolytes overestimate the capacity of their tools to grasp the scale and complexity of the human dynamics affecting the timing and acuity of the demands for services even in the life of one patient much less thousands, each of whom makes choices in their own lifeworld. Finance logic tends to miss the fact that intimate family and loved ones are key influencers in even the most basic decisions that affect the most obvious costs of one event. For instance, a man experiencing the earliest signs of a heart attack may or may not decide to say something and may or may not then agree to go to the emergency room. One factor may be the expense, but another might be their expectation of disrespect. One may know how to attribute costs to every bit of the machinery (the ambulance, the pills) but not the most crucial human factors.

It is fair to say that Nemesis blinds the institution so that it literally cannot see many of the most important things that drive the costs that matter most to them. The organization becomes ever more sensitive to the costs but oblivious to the complex web of human decisions driving costs. These ripples of complexity spread out quickly if one extrapolates the cycle of care (not just that one ambulance ride) at a community scale. The financial implications do not merely aggregate; they complexify in ways largely invisible to those charged with monitoring and reporting them to those charged with governing the institution over time. So, like a gathering storm, the unquestioned systemic logic accumulates in an inexorable process of self-reinforcement that seems inevitable. Nemesis comes.

Science Bent

Illich saw that the failure to advance overall health was not *despite* the health science establishment but *because* of it. The web of thought and practice that creates and replicates the institutions that provide care and manage prevention, guide research, educate professionals and promote the norms and basic paradigms of health science, simultaneously replicates patterns that operate in a manner that actively threatens the health of those whom they are supposed to serve. Illich saw the deep ironies and contradictions of medical health systems as a self-fulfilling and self-replicating reality that called forth the goddess *Nemesis*, who would exact retribution. If 'what goes around, comes around' then, as Illich saw, it is Nemesis who is coming for the whole web of institutions based on modern health sciences which have failed to deserve their extraordinary privileges.

Illich died in 2002, and it is more obvious with each passing year that he was right, at least in the United States, where well above 20 per cent of all economic activity now feeds the healthcare engine with singularly unimpressive outcomes. As a visiting Norwegian delegation observed, 'it is impressive how little you achieve with so much'.[6] It's not just the United States of America, however. In many parts of the world, the momentum of industrialized biomedical healthcare imperatives constantly threatens to absorb disproportionate funding, skills and attention, not infrequently to the detriment of other functional sectors such as housing, education, childcare and social services that impact health and are increasingly needed in our highly fluid postmodern reality. Interventional health science competes ferociously for resources and crowds out the other things that produce health.

Medicine Is Not Just Medical

Illich is important because the same phenomenon happens in other highly professionalized sectors that defend their privileges successfully against encroachment from others, even while failing to fulfil the greater good. Each makes it hard to imagine the resources, talent, energy and power distributed any other way. From any high building in any town one can see entire square miles where, at street level, life is often bitter, combative, filled with pain and unnecessarily short.

Why this overt disparity? It is not just the failure of the most expensive systems to provide their prescribed services; it is the irrelevance of those systems that absorb so much of available public and philanthropic funds and talent to deprive underpaid police, social services and those relevant to dependencies of many kinds. The science that justifies the specific service competes with the science that sees the whole community. The science is immature, contained in service of a privileged part while the whole suffers. Think, for example, of the wonders of prenatal imaging and surgical techniques on the one hand and, in exactly the same context, the reality of schools that can't afford to feed their hungry first graders.

Illich, in drawing on the image of Nemesis who hears the cries of the people, focused on the cruel implications of privilege and hubris for patients and those who *might have been* patients. And he focused on the implications of the imbalance of investments and talent that could rationally be ordered quite differently according to the health sciences to achieve the goals of widespread well-being. It is not science against everyone else; it is actually science against those who claim to serve it but use its credibility to serve limited self-interests, in effect, to the detriment if not against others.

Nemesis knows not only the painful edge of unmet human need, but the incomplete, borderline lazy analysis that leads to the clumsy policies that even fail on the crude measures of finance. Financial policies projected out of an unexamined view of how money works in actual social relationships at large scale can miss possibilities of efficiencies that more careful analysis would reveal.

People don't develop their medical conditions inside the medical systems. The people and their conditions come from neighbourhood systems that produce predictable long-term patterns of disease, social capacity and participation in financial systems of many kinds, only one of which is paying medical bills. It would often be more efficient and less costly to simply waive the cost for people from some predictable neighbourhoods because it is obvious that they cannot pay. Why add administrative costs to the relationship? Often the medical mercy sought is low cost – or should have been – when provided by a lower priced health professional. Even cheaper would be a part-time, neighbourhood-based community health worker who knows and is known by the neighbours and who could make available the medical care and preventive counsel that otherwise ends up in the costly point of hospital or emergency care much later, in a very predictable trajectory of suffering and cost.

Global Nemesis

The pattern of privilege and meagre outcomes in the U.S. healthcare environment is almost too easy a target for Illich. One place that you would think would get things right around the time of Illich's first writings was the mandate of primary healthcare adopted near the early days of the World Health Organization (WHO), still very much within the range of the influence of the visionary founders of the Christian Medical Commission at the World

Council of Churches in Geneva who provided decisive input to the WHO at the time.[7]

In 1978 at Alma-Ata, Kazakhstan, global leaders came together, tantalized by the possibility of building a global pattern of commitments that over time could result in *health for all*. It was so clear that science, even 50 years ago, could promise health for all if pursued with rigour and discipline through policies and practices focused on the prevention of conditions and affording access to very local primary healthcare to ensure early management of diseases. This was, of course, backstopped with integrated higher acute medical care when necessary and the promise of pharmaceuticals that even then could be projected to replace expensive interventions with regular management of conditions. So it was that the visionaries of Alma-Ata saw the possibility of medical sciences being brought to the tough streets and places where there are no streets through integrated partnerships with the social webs of faith, education and economic development that drive continual cycles of increased human well-being.

It did not happen. It was captured by medical privilege almost before the science-based alternative could get underway. As we suggested in our introduction, the problem began with the language and the underlying metaphorical trellis. Some focused more on *health* for all, trusting in the promise of medical sciences. Some focused more on health for *all*, trusting in the constantly accelerating power of community, especially when served by science. More than this, the righteous struggle embodied in the vision of the whole was lost almost immediately as the very earliest budgets were captured either by government ministries with other interests who did not understand the integrated science and settled for the more traditional pick-and-choose policies of 'selective primary health care'.[8] Most faith-based systems were already intellectually trapped by the problem of adapting or defending their expensive mission hospitals. They would have to fundamentally switch from interventional healthcare science to community health, which was no easier to do in Zambia than it was in North Carolina.

Illich was not the only one wondering if the healthcare establishment was entirely hopeless and so expensive as to be a threat to health of an entire generation of children. Jim Grant was the leader of UNICEF, the global organization for children, when he noticed that there was almost no relationship between the scale of the investment and elite qualifications in any particular programme and the achievement of children's health. The results seemed not only expensive but random.

Frustrated, he commissioned Carl Taylor, founding chair of International Health at Johns Hopkins University (also one of the main authors of the

Alma-Ata Declaration), and his son Daniel to examine successful interventions to determine if and how it was possible to mobilize the resting assets of the community to achieve what expensive centralized healthcare could not. The result was the body of logic and approach called SEED-SCALE.[9] We will comment on this model later in more detail, but here it is important to underline that the failure of 'health for all' is not because it's impossible at scale. Failure was not inevitable. It was a choice. And it was a failure not simply of budgets but of imagination. A failure to find a way that *was* possible, that *could* have unleashed the generative capacities of all so they would not merely be passive clients, patients or recipients of someone else's business model. This is what attracts the attention of Nemesis.

The Breaking Storm

Where do we see Nemesis today? Broken trust from privilege run amok damages every system and relationship it touches. But no system touches more lives with more painful injustice and failed mercy than the web of institutions built around health. As feminist bioethicist Charlene Galarneau reminds us, Dr Martin Luther King spoke of 'health, not health care; he said that this injustice is inhuman, rather than inhumane; and he named death as an outcome of injustice'. As she notes, the context in which he said this clarifies the point and the consequence he draws from it:

> We are concerned about the constant use of federal funds to support this most notorious expression of segregation [the racial segregation of hospitals]. Of all the forms of inequality, injustice in health is the most shocking and the most inhuman because it often results in physical death. I see no alternative to direct action and *creative nonviolence to raise the conscience of the nation.*[10]

It is far too easy to think that Dr King thought the answer was simply erasing the financial or policy barriers blocking entrance into the doors of the care providers, or even giving more balanced funding to the public health structures most involved with the neighbourhoods of colour. Tuned to the more complex interwoven nature of the patterns that produce disparate suffering generation after generation, King was quite close to Illich in seeing patterns and outcomes so lacking in mercy as systemic and thus self-replicating. He saw the self-reinforcing weave of privileges, of race and class, of legal status, of gender and of the long momentum of accumulated wealth and educational advantages. It is that long pattern, not the specific event, that attracts Nemesis.

If it were merely a set of complicated causal drivers, it would be possible for a group of well-intentioned and thoughtful people to map a different way. This is why we need to stop, break the momentum and look at our own entanglement in the systems of privilege before we leap to fixing things. See the whole, not just its complicatedness but in its complexity, which is something else entirely; then move towards deep accountability.

And what is the *whole* thing? The failure of the healthcare establishment lies precisely in thinking of itself apart from the larger community systems. It functions in practice, if not in theory, all too often largely as if it is an isolated system when in fact it is only one among a range of other interlocking social bodies.

Alma-Ata saw precisely that reality and promised an approach to all that is surely less expensive than our current non-system. In many ways there was no more well-intentioned and well-qualified group in the history of the health sciences to do just that than the group that gathered at Alma-Ata, whose vision became ensnared almost before it started.

Don't blame science and don't blame arithmetic. Nemesis is coming for us, not just in anger but driven by sorrow for the lost opportunities that would allow everyone to participate in making possible health for all, for tragically failed decisions that hurt people unfairly and entangle one inside systems that constrain bold action.

We should not be surprised that so many people in so many places grow in anger, fear and despair at their treatment (or lack of it) and their exclusion or alienation from the systems and their experts that dominate their social reality. This is easy to manipulate by self-interested actors into storms that spin into many other sectors that affect people's lives, driving predictable political weirdness. People who inhabit the self-interested centres of power and money are not shy intentionally to leverage this rage and despair to mobilize populist movements for their own gain, happily propagating uncertainty and emphasizing the limits of science (whose method rests on uncertainty anyway) to sow doubt and confusion where it suits them, employing ideological and religious legitimations in disingenuous ways to further their ends. For them, rage, fear and despair are manna – not from heaven but from hell – food for a new breed of autocrats, plutocrats and oligarchs whose aims are not aligned with the vast majority of people from whom they draw their living or against whom they build walls and machines of war and repression.

Lest we simply look away from ourselves, we ought never to forget to notice our own complicities. We are reminded of this, all too disturbingly, by Bertolt Brecht's instructive play, *Saint Joan of the Stockyards*, written almost a hundred years ago. In it, Brecht highlights the deep ambiguities that embroil everyone:

the owners of the Chicago stockyards, the workers in them and Joan and her Black Straw Hats Mission to the workers. All were caught up in the systemic distortions of their various relationships. Joan seeks to confront Pierpont Mauler, the mega-tycoon of the stockyards, with the moral challenge of the hard life and conditions of the workers, whose interests are not served by his. Gradually her good intentions, driven by religious motivations, seep into the heart of Mauler. Mauler is personally moved and sympathetic, but nothing really changes. Her efforts are all in vain, regularly thwarted, not so much by bad intentions but by the restrictive logic of the institutional relationships that govern the business and its interactions with those who work for it. In the end, there is no resolution, and Joan dies a bitter and cynical martyr.

It did, and does, not have to be this way. In the face of what threatens us, we tend to forget how much we know about finding our way through difficult, depressing, anxiety-fomenting, soul-sucking, hope-chilling stuff. *Death is not the only story, far from it; life is at work too.* What's more, it's not without serious strength. Spinning complex webs of vitality, infusing and energizing all it touches, it breaks forth in unexpected and surprising ways. It suggests and prefigures other kinds of relationships than those that are captive to anger, fear and self-interest as not only possible, not only urgently necessary, but as within reach and, in some places, as already at work.

That's where we need to look, to life, for clues to a deeply accountable way forward. To do so, however, we need to rethink our linear ways of understanding complex realities – like the life of human beings. It is important not to participate in the passive despair that the momentum is irreversible, that things must work as they have. If that were so, we would be at the bar, not at the keyboard.

In this chapter, we have used healthcare organizations as one lens on the storm. But Illich would be the first to warn that identical patterns, dynamics and momentum of self-serving privilege are present in most institutional networks. Every single thing humans make or unmake, do or undo emerges from a system. Those systems usually stabilize into a network of privilege that can function over time in the same way healthcare organizations have evolved. Because these are not closed systems but ones that flow into others, let us not treat them in isolation, as if their problems and challenges can be dealt with piecemeal.

As one step in that direction, we turn now to the question of value, what gives rise to it and where it lies in the political economies that have so much to do with our health and well-being. This will set the ground for a different way of thinking and acting that we regard as central to living out of an imperative of deep accountability.

Notes

1 Rainer Maria Rilke, 'The Beholder (Der Schauende)', in *Selected Poems of Rainer Maria Rilke* (Harper & Row, 1981), 105; translation by Robert Bly, mildly adjusted.

2 Donella H. Meadows et al., *The Limits to Growth: A Report for the Club of Rome's Project on the Predicament of Mankind* (Universe Books, 1972).

3 Ivan Illich, *Medical Nemesis: The Expropriation of Health* (Calder & Boyars, 1975).

4 For example, see his early critique of the domination of technocratic elites in Ivan Illich, *Tools of Conviviality* (Harper and Row, 1973).

5 See Jürgen Habermas, *The Theory of Communicative Action Vol. 2: Lifeworld and System: A Critique of Functionalist Reason* (Beacon Press, 1987).

6 Personal note.

7 James C. McGilvray, *The Quest for Health and Wholeness* (German Institute for Medical Mission (Difäm), 1981).

8 Marcos Cueto, 'The Origins of Primary Health Care and Selective Primary Health Care', *American Journal of Public Health* 94, no. 11 (November 2004): 1864–74.

9 Daniel C. Taylor, and Carl E. Taylor, *Just and Lasting Change: When Communities Own Their Futures*, 2nd ed. (Johns Hopkins University Press, 2016 [2002]); see also Daniel Taylor-Ide and Carl E. Taylor, *Community-Based Sustainable Human Development* (New York: UNICEF, 1995), https://cdn.future.edu/wp-content/uploads/2018/06/1995 -02-community-based-sustainable-human-development.pdf.

10 Charlene Galarneau, 'King's Words on Health Injustice: What Did He Actually Say?' *Official Blog: International Journal of Feminist Approaches to Bioethics*, 19 April 2018, https://www.ijfab.org/blog/2018/04/kings-words-on-health-injustice-what-did-he -actually-say/.

Chapter 5

VALUE

Value guides claims of time,
attention, money, place, privilege.
Value, wrongly given, guarantees everything going wrong.

How do we know what to do? What is the most important – valuable – thing in which to invest our creativity, sweat and time? How do we know the value of any particular service, product or activity? Economists tend to keep it simple: the more costly something is, the more valuable it is. However, a casual stroll down any market street provides a daily deluge of silly ornaments that often cost a great deal; life and death necessities they are not. And the most valuable things are not monetized at all: What is the cost of a mother's priceless love?

A critical component of deep accountability, then, is to accept responsibility for clarifying value. Our whole society is structured to give value to some things and people instead of others. We are told by means of their price whose contributions to the well-being and flourishing of society are valuable, and whose are not. These narratives follow and reinforce each other like caribou hooves pounding the same trail when better ones are there. The stories of value touch almost every sphere of our life together: work and home, learning and study, play and recreation, income and status. They affect how we craft our social systems and what kind of institutions we protect and strengthen. The stories teach us about our dignity and value as persons.

Value is much more than price, but you don't have to go further than prices to discern the warped story we are told about where value is located, acknowledged and rewarded. A soccer or basketball star sitting on the bench may be valued far beyond entire villages in many parts of the world. CEOs across the Fortune 500 companies 'earn' hundreds, even thousands of times the average worker's income, which in the United States has fallen below inflation increases.[1]

Such radical disparities, echoed in societies across the world, are not simply the result of individual opportunities, preferences, actions and talents. They represent a fundamentally skewed reality. Economist Mariana Mazzucato of University College London points to them as indicators of seriously misplaced conceptions of value. Plato, she reminds us, disliked myths about ill-behaved gods. She thinks we are now captive to an equally ill-behaved 'modern myth, about value creation in the economy'. So, she calls us to rethink what has value, how it is acknowledged or rewarded. As she notes, this 'is not an abstract debate but one with far-reaching consequences – social and political as well as economic – for everyone'.[2]

Who Creates Value?

As a defining event of recent times, the Covid-19 pandemic was a morality tale about value. The coronavirus took many lives even as it ripped away the deceptive surface of much of our globalized political economy, exposing its conflicts and structural vulnerabilities. It revealed the extent to which the lives of rich, powerful, influential and celebrated people claim value that is built to a large extent on illusions about a crucial dichotomy: who *creates* and who *takes* value. The pandemic clarified that many other people who had been undervalued and earned far less were genuinely essential.

One particularly telling activity marked Covid-19. In city after city across the world, people came out to stand on their balconies or lean out of windows to clap their hands or bang rhythmically on potlids, expressing their gratitude for the exhausted, emotionally stressed and personally endangered healthcare workers who were caring for them and their loved ones in hospitals and clinics. Before then, those underpaid and overworked people had mostly been invisible, regarded in the 'old normal' as being in some way of lower status and supposed value than the elites.

They were not the only ones suddenly seen as essential. Under lockdowns and in quarantine people turned gratefully to those who supplied assistance, providing transport, delivering food, medicines and personal items and much else besides. In offices and service centres, over and over again, others carried the extra burdens that sick, absent colleagues left hanging, even as many of them were retrenched in the face of collapsing businesses affected by the pandemic. It wasn't just employed people who did what was needed, however. Friends, neighbours and helpful strangers found themselves taking on responsibilities beyond the norm, joining together in new initiatives to support members of their community.

In the process it began to dawn on many people that CEOs, celebrities and their like – the icons of financial capital, the captains of industry, the cheerleaders of the consumer economy and the marketers of status were takers, not creators. The truly essential members of society, whom we are once again in danger of overlooking, are far less obvious and far more widespread, inhabiting all corners of our life together.

Value is Power

Value gives power to claims of time, attention, money, place, privilege. Things of ultimate value may even wrongly justify violence to take from another or defend against inconvenient claims for mercy. Decisions about value can be profound or trivial: how the Supreme Court values legal precedent, or how the church committee discerns how to let the children of the neighbourhood whom 'God so loves' gain access to what they need, or gives time to picking out the colour of the carpet. The structures through which power flows in organizational life tell us everything about what that organization assigns value. Time, voice, budget, presence and visibility all reflect power exerted on behalf of that which is found valuable.

Value, wrongly given, guarantees everything going wrong. Value accurately awarded makes it possible for people and systems to make decisions that lead to life. To explore this more fully, here in relation to the substantial systems and structures governing our life together that we call polity and economy, we turn to Mariana Mazzucato and her seminal work, *The Value of Everything: Making and Taking in the Global Economy*.

Mazzucato asks us to be conscious and critical of our unspoken assumptions about who really is essential, that is, who actually creates value. We may think that economists have thought all this through. Mazzucato, however, with the moral clarity of Illich, argues that modern economics has lost its way and has helped us lose ours – by failing its most basic task of thinking carefully about value. Contrary to a long history of economic thinking that linked value to real goods, the contemporary era has reframed value as resting on money, in effect, on price. If you are rich or earning a high income relative to others, then you and your work are valuable. If you are neither rich nor earning an income, then you are of lesser or no value, at least as far as your contribution to society is concerned. Price determines value, and the market is where it is measured. This, notes Mazzucato, 'has made it easier for value-*extracting* activities to masquerade as value-*creating* activities'.[3]

This story, she says, is fundamentally wrong, and it was not always this way. There was a time when economists told a very different story about the measure of value. Over time the defining story we are told has changed, reversing the relationship between value and price that the classical economists, including Adam Smith and Karl Marx, understood very differently. The objective idea of value long at the heart of economics – that it rests on a creative activity of some kind or another, not on the extraction of value provided by others – shifted in the twentieth century towards a subjective focus on 'concepts of "scarcity" and "preferences"', thereby introducing a 'swing from value determining price to price determining value'.[4]

At least two effects of this shift are significant. First, it 'allows someone with massive wealth to claim they are the producers of value even though they do nothing but manipulate financial markets [...]'. Second, it strips down what was understood as a *political* economy to mere economics. Consequently, it is paraded as a science rather than a human endeavour, which removes any consideration of will, especially political will, from its calculations. This exclusion of will is seriously reductionist, leaving aside the fact that econometrics and mathematical formulas give us a far from certain grasp of economic realities, as is obvious from the radically different judgements various economists come to about the same 'facts'. As Mazzucato sardonically puts it:

> So while economics students used to get a rich and varied education in the idea of value, learning what different schools of economic thought had to say about it, today they are taught only that value is determined by the dynamics of price, due to scarcity and preferences. This is not presented as a particular theory of value – just as Economics 101 [...].[5]

Price is *not* the measure of all things, she notes. It reduces value to a radically instrumental view of markets and money. In the process, it erases the human being as such. Put differently, it hides the asymmetries of power – the question of who makes decisions, how they are made and to what ends – that actively shape markets all the time. This convenient erasure of the political dimension of the economy serves particularly well those who have the greatest power in it. Simultaneously, it allows great harm to come to those who don't.

Thinking Differently

Mazzucato gives us three reasons to rethink value. One is that those who make policy are inevitably influenced, consciously or unconsciously, by ideas about value in 'setting a direction' for any particular institution or society, thus 'deciding which activities are more important than others'.[6] For example, Gary worked for a hospital that, like many, was carefully tuned to public relations, never missing an opportunity for the shiny brochure or photo op. During the pandemic, it raised millions from the community to support the 'essential' nurses and healthcare frontliners. But as the crisis passed, it regressed to more traditional priorities – a half billion-dollar surgical tower rises while across campus it quietly bulldozes homes that could have been converted for the low-wage essential workers who it knew slept in their cars. It knows the prices of the services it can sell but forgets what and who is valued most.

A second reason to rethink value is that clarity about who creates value has 'massive implications for one particular area: the distribution of income between different members of society'.[7] The turn in our time to a price-based theory of value, in her view, is in fact 'a major reason for wealth often being distributed in dysfunctional ways'. If your value is determined solely by the price of your contribution, well, then, it makes sense that a high-powered influencer on TikTok is 'worth' the millions they derive from being special or interesting. Price equals value. It's much more likely that your discomfort is well-placed: You don't like the basic theory of value that undergirds this kind of economy. A different theory of value at this point is not just helpful but, as we see it, vitally necessary.

The third reason to reinstate a theory of value is perhaps the most fundamental of all: the fact that 'the disappearance of value from the economic debate hides what *should be alive, public and actively contested*'.[8] Because value is no longer part of the debate, determinations about the most crucial dimensions of the economy – who it serves, how and to what ends – are delegated to an elite band of economists whose privilege rests on their claim that their decisions are in the best interests of all.

The economists have become a new kind of priesthood whose authority rests on the claim that *they* understand the 'science' of economics. Alongside them are the corporate elites and their political clients who avoid any transparent or extended public input on their enterprises and activities. Instead, the paradigm of marginal utility drives their understanding of value. Its doctrines – dogmas, actually – of 'scarcity' and 'preferences',[9] expressed via price (governed by supply and demand factors) in a market free of interference, are assumed to be as natural as gravity. For them, the market sets the price and is thus the source of value and the primary end of all decisions.

Absurd Prices, Lost Value

The consequences of the reduction of value to price are profound even as they border on the absurd. Mazzucato gives an example that is easy to grasp and close to home, quite literally. In current thinking the value produced by housework is not counted, hence, not seen as value added. Under 'price determines value' thinking, '[...] [i]f we paid our neighbours to look after our children and do our laundry, and they paid us to do theirs', their value would be added.[10] Do that work ourselves, however, then the theory assumes no value is added because no money has changed hands. This is clearly absurd.

The same would apply to unpaid care or any other service that does not directly generate income. Much of what communities do, for example, to contribute to the health of the members, whether by helping people from one place to another, providing meals or helping complete necessary forms and so on, would similarly be regarded as having no value by virtue of generating no income or having no price.

In this logic a community health worker employed by a hospital adds value, but someone doing exactly the same work in the community without pay adds no value. By contrast, a hedge fund manager who simply shifts money around to make more money is regarded as productive because even if no value of any other kind is added, the price has increased (it can, of course, decrease just as quickly). As that highly successful investor George Soros freely concedes, this is mere casino capitalism. Of course, the complicated arithmetic can easily hide the most obvious things. A great deal that we all regard as having value simply disappears from sight when we let the price of things be untethered from a theory of value.

Removing the question of value from the public sphere is a historical shift that is not inevitable. It was very different in earlier streams of thought that Mazzucato acutely describes, from the Mercantilists to the Physiocrats, from Adam Smith and David Ricardo to Karl Marx, among others. Smith, for example, frequently lauded by market fundamentalists, was anything but sanguine about markets. He understood how distorted they could be, how bereft of moral imperatives of any kind, for which reason he spent a great deal of energy in seeking a moral ground to constrain the effects of unbridled or instrumentalized markets.[11] This concern rather disappears when it comes to the rise of the modern neoclassical economists and, especially, what Mazzucato calls the 'colossus' of financial capital and its high priests.

Here she introduces the fateful and influential theory of shareholder value that Milton Friedman and others champion: that the only legitimate social responsibility corporations have is to their shareholders. This is a huge shift, for which she gives a paradigmatic example. The head of IBM in 1968 described its three major priorities as respect for individual employees, a commitment to customer service and achieving excellence. Fifty years later, however, IBM's president stated that its main aim was simply to double earnings per share over the next five years.[12] It's easy to see that a completely different understanding of value is at work (specifically, who and what kind of work is valued). It's also easy to see, Mazzucato makes clear, that 'value is not a given thing […]; it is shaped and created'.

That's a very important message. If value was repeatedly shaped and created in one or another way before, then it can be done again. It will not depend upon mathematical formulas and data mining but on will – public will as much as any. Thus, the question of value must not be hidden but must be drawn into the 'alive, public and actively contested' engagement Mazzucato calls for. Mazzucato, the economist, is clear that value is too important to leave in the hands of economists. Value tells us how to invest not just our money but our sweat, tears, joy, time and affection to the thriving of the human mesh.

Disrespect – and Dignity

We may love to watch Lionel Messi outwit a defender and think he is worth his weight in gold (at 148 pounds, his net worth of $850 million in 2024 was in fact about 257 times his weight in gold). This is extracted, not created wealth, even as others who earn barely enough to survive create wealth for which they get little credit. In our time, increasingly so, an extremely small number of individuals or families, across the board and in the great majority of countries, wield an astronomically high percentage of available wealth, accordingly exercising an inordinately large influence over matters that affect us all. They represent the unprecedented rise of financial capital, whose role is all too easily taken to be completely normal and justifiable when it really conceals a historical shift that hides a great deal.

As Mazzucato spells out over three chapters,[13] financial capital was once seen largely as 'unearned income' (or in an earlier era, usury). Now even corporations producing traditional material goods such as cars offer their own financing, to the point where their gains from it are greater than the value of the sales of the products they make. Meanwhile, venture capital entrepreneurs, hedge funds and other agencies utilize new financial instruments, often opaque, such as derivatives, credit-swaps or share buybacks, to make money off money. In the process, we have seen an astonishing shift of vast sums moving away from investment in objective productive activities to non-productive enrichment, that is, for the extraction of value rather than the creation of it. This has produced a remarkably small set of individuals who have become super-rich.

As suggested by a recent edition of the German magazine, *Der Spiegel*,[14] this represents a neo-feudal aristocracy, more precisely, a global plutocracy. Its members are able, among other things, to wield armies of lobbyists to promote their interests or a host of advisers and lawyers to help them evade an appropriate contribution to the taxes otherwise able to support social programmes and safety net policies for those who need them. They are also able to use their money and influence to extract large portions of government budgets with little return to the public or the common good or, in some parts of the world, to circumvent any legal or political difficulties in that regard simply by capturing the state.

So it is that in many parts of the world we see rising anger at those who sit in the commanding heights of polity and economy, not infrequently engaging in obnoxious displays of wealth and status, even as they do all they can to protect their self-interest at the cost of others. The 'elites' is a common word expressing this antipathy on the part of those who feel shut out of the economy or its future. Canny politicians have been able to use it to their own ends, often drawing on nationalistic or jingoist ideologies to incite and mobilize the populace against their presumed enemies or competitors. Globalization, in this context, becomes a swear word.

Part of what evokes anger, especially in places like the United States (but not only), is what Harvard professor Michael Sandel calls 'the tyranny of merit'. It's linked to the question of value. Two particular aspects of what people who feel shut out of the benefits of globalization experience are what Sandel describes as a 'technocratic way of conceiving the public good' and a 'meritocratic way of defining winners and losers'.[15]

The first is closely related to the role of economic and other 'experts' in determining value not by means of its contribution to the common good but through price and its calculus. It fits neatly with the view that public goods provided by government, especially social supports, are generally inefficient (a beloved term) and should be curtailed as far as possible. It also dovetails with the conviction that the market, understood in instrumental terms as a neutral or impartial mechanism for regulating supply and demand, should determine value. On this reading, market value equals social contribution. Highlighting the moral absurdity of this idea, Sandel gives the example of Walter White, the gifted high school chemistry teacher in the television series *Breaking Bad*, who makes millions on the drug market, way beyond his pay as a teacher. As Sandel says, 'most would agree, however that his contribution as a teacher has far greater value than his contribution as a drug dealer'.[16]

This distorted market version of reality leaves little space for democratic participation by the people most affected by its prescriptions. The whole system is opaque, excluding the average person from either understanding or contributing to decisions made. Public discourse is hollowed out in the process, moral and political judgement outsourced to experts or technocrats, and democratic argument of meaning and purpose emptied.[17] If people do understand and don't like what they see, then little outlet exists for their anger or sense of alienation. Instead, they are likely to feel disempowered and disrespected as far as their contribution to society is concerned. As Sandel puts it, this is 'not the result of inexorable forces' but, as Mazzucato might say, it is a consequence of how value is constituted in the institutions that are most central to our lives.

The second aspect Sandel highlights takes us even further into the murky pits of this situation, for it impacts directly on a sense of worth as a human being, that is, on the question of dignity. Meritocracy gives social standing and esteem to those regarded as having greater merit, understood in terms of credentials suited to a technocratic or market-value society. This elevation of merit simultaneously depreciates the contributions of most workers and erodes their social standing and esteem,[18] with a corresponding shrinking of one's sense of worth and dignity. That this fuels a backlash should not surprise us. As Sandel neatly puts it,

> Being good at making money measures neither our merit nor the value of our contribution. All the successful can honestly say is that they have managed – through some unfavourable mix of genius or guile, timing or talent, luck or pluck or grim determination – to cater effectively to the jumble of wants and desires, however weighty or frivolous, that constitute consumer demand at any given moment. Satisfying consumer demand is not valuable in itself; its value depends, case-by-case, on the moral status of the ends it serves.[19]

Hidden in Plain Sight: Working with a Different Story

A better reflection of reality, a better 'story', places value before price, value creation above value extraction. The creation of value, Mazzucato points out, is far from being just the work of shareholders or owners of capital and money. It is a complex and deeply collective process, involving a much wider range of stakeholders than usually acknowledged.

A fully accountable participant view focuses on the web of social relationships, paid or unpaid, that actually produce value, with goals that go well beyond mere finance and its calculus. It 'sees people not just as inputs but as essential contributors who need to be nurtured. Trust – critical for any enterprise – is then built in [...]'.[20] One could go further to say, as we do, that a complete theory of value includes not just the web of social relationships with other human beings, as vital as they are. It also includes, as many indigenous peoples around the world know, our relationship to nature, to the earth that sustains and the creatures that are part of the ecosystem we inhabit, upon which we depend far more than we have long thought under conditions of modernity.

The functional labour we need to do differently is valuing what's really valuable. We outsource this process too easily and get it all wrong in the process. It's actually the fundamental responsibility of a grown-up. And they are not necessarily experts. It requires a different understanding of what counts, being fully aware that not everything that can be measured actually counts and that not everything that counts can be measured. Our technocratic, meritocratic culture is obsessed with measurement but, as Donella Meadows so clearly expressed it, 'No one can precisely define or measure justice, democracy, security, freedom, truth, or love.'[21]

Meadows, of course, was a crucial part of the group that produced the 1972 Club of Rome Report on *The Limits to Growth*.[22] That's 50 years ago. Now, at a time when many of the warnings given then are no longer warnings but a part of our reality, we face an even more urgent scenario. Simply to rely on a market-based theory of scarcity and preferences – which challenges neither the ideology of unlimited growth nor the hubris associated with a belief that technology will save us – is no solution. What matters more and more, as Carlos Alvarez Pereira, co-author of the Club of Rome's new book, *Limits and Beyond*, reminds us, is realizing that a healthy life and the well-being of all depends fundamentally on 'the quality of our relationships with other humans, with nature […]'.

What does this actually mean for us? It means turning our attention to what Pereira sees as 'an ongoing cultural change often hidden in plain sight', one that is 'less obvious, less evident, less in the headlines', experiments that are being conducted largely at the local community level but with ramifications well beyond any particular community. In his view, 'The human revolution is already happening – it's just that we don't see it.' If he is right, even if the odds are large and the countervailing forces substantial, then we need to look for where this is happening, in our terms, for where life is breaking forth.

Organizing Around True Value

The question of value is exactly what Jim Grant, for 15 years an executive director of UNICEF, was asking when he noticed the disconnect between how much funding it invested in a project that was supposed to help children and what actually came out. Described as 'a little-known American aid worker' who had 'probably saved more lives than were destroyed by Hitler, Mao, and Stalin combined',[23] Grant recognized that the normal management system simply did not tell him how to get better results. More money might help, but what and who should one spend it on? What is truly valuable – worthy – of the children?

As we noted in the previous chapter, he turned to a trusted friend for help, to Carl Taylor and his son Daniel, whom Jim Grant knew had been formed in the crucible of selfless mission work in Asia, just as he had been. Grant needed to have confidence in the deep-in-the-bones values of those he now entrusted with the question of value. He also had some money for plane tickets, which gave the Taylors the capacity to conduct a research process involving hundreds of people on every inhabited continent. They engaged with and listened to expertise of all kinds, formal and informal, drawing on a variety of metrics and wide-ranging testimony.

After four years, they produced the radical process called SEED-SCALE, laid out in peer-reviewed publications, that dared to promise 'just and lasting social change'.[24] The process saw value quite differently than traditional – even current! – development experts who were dependent on different paths of power. Even with the imprimatur of UNICEF and the Taylors' impeccable Hopkins/Harvard academic credentials, the SEED-SCALE process did not change the field. Indeed, Grant counselled that their vision of value was too radical for the normal academic institutional establishment. They created a tiny but scrappy new 'Future Generations University' instead, with a prescient URL: future.org. Illich would smile.

What happens when you value different things? One begins with power, intelligence and energy at the bottom, on the ground that sustains those who are not the beneficiaries of dominant powers and extractive privileges. SEED-SCALE especially values the mesh of affection, dignity and respect one finds in the smallest villages, usually nurtured by the women who hope for their children and will do anything, learn anything for them. The Taylors began with what the mothers knew, adding at first only a process for them to see the pattern that might lead to a better life in the survival of the children. Carl called this the Child Survival Revolution,[25] but its apparent simplicity hid a far more evolved (*involved*) process that included a sophisticated system of gathering and analysing data to empower the 'affective mesh' (our phrase; see Chapter 7) to systematically guide how the existing powers, including government and intermediary organizations, could be involved without crushing the process.

SEED-SCALE includes as crucial people at the base, in the community, owning the valuation, deciding what is of value and testing it out, not primarily dependent on fixed models or mere checklists but, as in Carl Taylor's interest, accountable first to the mothers and everyone else involved in the lives of the children. Only then does one include in a systematic way the management and involvement of those from centres of expertise and power such as UNICEF or a mission agency. Then ensuring that the process does meet those standards.

Accurate valuing of who and what matters most to the people takes us into the heart of being deeply accountable for the dynamism of the liquid whole.[26] The sophisticated approach is still radical enough that it lies almost entirely outside the normal discussion of global health (even while honouring the Taylors personally with all sorts of awards). The Taylors were not infrequently cranky at the disingenuous embrace of valuable ideas by people who spoke the language but failed to follow them into practice.

Mazzucato promises that we can be worthy of the world we love if we are bold enough to see value clearly. This does not mean that the world will turn and follow. Bill McKibben, in calling Daniel Taylor the most interesting development expert he has ever met, describes SEED-SCALE in much the way Mazzucato might wish we could describe other components of modern systems: 'Forget big plans. Development is not a product, not a target, not some happy future state […] it's a process, measured not in budgets but in how we invest our human energy'.[27]

One way to think of how this energy unfolds, of how life works we would say, is to consider the concept of involution.

Notes

1 See Andrew Marquardt, 'CEO Pay Is Skyrocketing as the Average Worker Struggles to Keep Up With Inflation. Here's Who Got the Biggest Rises', *Fortune*, 4 April 2022, https://fortune.com/2022/04/04/median-ceo-pay-amazon-discovery-raises; AFL-CIO, 'Highest-Paid CEOs', accessed 10 December 2024, https://aflcio.org/executive-paywatch/highest-paid-ceos.

2 Mariana Mazzucato, *The Value of Everything: Making and Taking in the Global Economy* (Hachette, 2018), xviii.

3 Ibid., xviii (our emphases).

4 Ibid., 7.

5 Ibid., 8.

6 Ibid., 13.

7 Ibid., 12.

8 Ibid., 11 (our emphasis).

9 This is not an essay in economic theory, of course; for a full discussion of these points, see Mazzucato, *The Value of Everything*, ch. 2: 'Value in the Eye of the Beholder: The Rise of the Marginalists', 57–74.

10 Ibid., 92.

11 For an accessible discussion of Smith's concern for morality, in which he moved somewhat away from both utilitarianism and consequentialism (exciting Immanuel Kant's interest), see Arthur Herman, *How the Scots Invented the Modern World: The True Story of How Western Europe's Poorest Nation Created Our World and Everything in It* (Crown, 2001), 197ff.

12 Mazzucato, *The Value of Everything*, 179.

13 Ibid., 161–269, chapters on 'Financialization of the Real Economy', 'Extracting Value Through the Innovation Economy', and 'Undervaluing the Public Sector'.

14 Tim Bartz, Christoph Giessen, Marc Pitzke, Michael Sauga and Thomas Schultz, 'Die feudalistische Welt der Superreichen' (trans. 'The feudalistic world of the super-rich'), *Der Spiegel*, 20 May 2022, Nr 21.

15 Michael J. Sandel, *The Tyranny of Merit: What's Become of the Common Good?* (Allen Lane, 2020), 19.

16 Ibid., 139.

17 Ibid., 29–31.

18 Ibid., 29.

19 Ibid., 140.

20 Mazzucato, *The Value of Everything*, 184–5.

21 Donella Meadows, 'Dancing With Systems', *The Donella Meadows Project: Academy for Systems Change*, 2002, https://donellameadows.org/archives/dancing-with-systems.

22 Donella H. Meadows et al., *The Limits to Growth: A Report for the Club of Rome's Project on the Predicament of Mankind* (Universe Books, 1972); also Wikipedia, 'The Limits to Growth', https://en.wikipedia.org/wiki/The_Limits_to_Growth.

23 Nicholas Kristof, 'Good News: Karlo Will Live', *New York Times*, March 6 2008, https://www.nytimes.com/2008/03/06/opinion/06kristof.html.

24 Taylor and Taylor, *Just and Lasting Change* (2016); see also https://seed-scale.org.

25 See https://iris.who.int/bitstream/handle/10665/62644/WHO_UNICEF_HED _85.7.pdf; also Richard Horton, 'Offline: A New Revolution for Child and Adolescent Health', *The Lancet* 399, no. 10336 (2022): P1679, https://doi.org/10.1016/S0140 -6736(22)00739-5.

26 For what we mean by the liquid whole, see Zygmunt Bauman's connected works, *Liquid Modernity* (Polity Press, 2000); *Liquid Love: On the Frailty of Human Bonds* (Polity Press, 2003); *Liquid Times: Living in an Age of Uncertainty* (Polity Press, 2006).

27 Bill McKibben, *Deep Economy: The Wealth of Communities and the Durable Future* (Henry Holt, 2007), 211.

Chapter 6

INVOLUTION

Since Darwin wrote two centuries ago, no idea has been more powerful in understanding change than evolution. Everything in this view, including all human systems, evolves over time from that which precedes it. If evolution was long disputed, nothing appears more obvious now. Yet we have been missing a fundamental point. Only very recently, an equally powerful idea has emerged: Change is not just about *e*volution, but also *in*volution.

The idea of involution, we shall see, is more than helpful at a time when so many parts of our political and organizational systems are seeking to pull back into their defensive boundaries, their leaders using privilege and power to distance us from that which we fear in the 'other' whom we do not know or understand. This is encouraged by a simplistic version of evolution dumbed down into the survival of the fittest or the most the powerful. Involution, by contrast, is disorientingly positive: It invites us to find our path forward into highly complex interdependent relationships. We find ourselves *among* others, not against others or they against us.

This has great implications for organizing our daily work differently. Before we can see how powerful involution is to our work in the world, we need to be sure we understand it well. Let's look briefly, then, at how we might work out of involution logic to vexing problems so you can sense how useful this is to the desire to be deeply accountable.

It helps to think of involution in contrast to evolution, the concept to which it relates. Evolution is of course a well-established metaphor, one we are most likely to adopt consciously or unconsciously whenever we think of the development of a child into an adult and beyond, of the flow of generations in an extended family, or of the elaboration of increasingly sophisticated forms of social organization (there are no guarantees here; evolution, not equivalent to 'progress', includes unproductive changes and dead-ends).

Involution, as Merlin Sheldrake describes it, is less sequential, less about successive changes built on earlier ones and far more about the constant forming and re-forming of relationships that enable cooperation rather than competition, in which none are able to hijack the relationships for their own exclusive benefit.[1] Sheldrake also describes involution as associations that help us go outside and beyond our prior limits, and while this is important in helping us break free of unproductive or dead-end situations, our most common associations with each other are in groups, institutions or organizations defined not by what's outside them but by what's *inside*. They set limits on belonging and we love those limits because they give us a sense of community, security and identity. It matters not if it's a sports team, an ethnic, religious or cultural tradition, an ideology or membership in an elite fellowship or private club. The impulse is to distinguish between who is in and who is out. To wander outside and beyond their prior limits is discouraged, perhaps gently, perhaps through penalty, expulsion or worse. Rare are those bodies to which we belong that encourage an expansion inclusion of others. So, we have to explain why we think deep accountability lies elsewhere, literally off the normal map.

On Not Dumbing Down Life

Neil Young, writes David Samuels, who interviewed him for the *New York Times Magazine*, 'is crankier than a hermit being stung by bees. [...] He hates what digital technology is doing to music'. He thinks that 'substituting smoothed-out algorithms for the contingent complexity of biological existence' is actually 'bad for us [...], an insult to the human mind and the human soul'.[2] What Young wants is 'the promise of the real': the richness of sound that digitalization cannot reproduce; but also, crucially, the missed notes, the off-kilter resonance, the ever-present acceptance of imperfection.

If Young is cranky, so too is our friend Paul Laurienti, a brilliant neuroscientist who spends most of his days directing a cutting-edge research institute on complex brain networks at a well-known medical school. Paul is annoyed by the dumbed-down version of brain science that focuses on developing more and more granular maps of the brain. He readily concedes that mapping the brain at the finest possible level is what he spends most of his professional life doing with his colleagues and students, using the most advanced technologies and software to observe and measure neuroelectric or neurochemical interactions in the brain, linking specific regions to particular kinds of activities.

This has led to an understanding of the brain that was unimaginable to the early pioneers who had to rely on far cruder instruments. But Paul believes the process has created an intellectual dead-end that has not produced any truly revolutionary changes in neuroscience since the 1700s when Franz Joseph Gall discovered localization in the brain, and Korbinian Brodmann in the nineteenth century produced a schematic map of the regions of the brain still largely in use today. Paul certainly accepts that this kind of localized map of regions of the brain is not entirely wrong and that there are definable, specialized areas such as the visual cortex, for example, that do reflect specific activities of the brain.

That's not really the problem. When hiking, it is important to have a map, but also to realize that the map is not the dirt, the pathway or the mountain. It is a representation of part of reality that completely elides a great deal that is also present. In short, a highly granular map of the brain may encourage us to think we know more about the phenomenon than we do.

So, Paul asks, do *perceptions* occur in a particular region? What's going on when a song gets stuck in our head? Do we even know what a *thought* is? We haven't any idea, actually. No one has figured it out. Why not?

It's the perspective that is too narrow, all too simplistic for Paul. Brain scientists do use network theory, including Paul, but as he experiences it, mostly simply to reframe localization in a more complicated way. Brain areas aren't like billiard balls whose mass, velocity, acceleration and trajectory you can track. In complex systems, the cause and effect are not always linear. The same causes may have different effects depending on the state of the system, which is always changing. A brain presents an infinite and dynamic number of possibilities, which are very hard to study. It's simply not possible to get off and stop the roundabout (actually more like a soft tornado that goes where it will). No one brain region causes you to do something, as Paul sees it. Every region matters. Individual brain areas are ultimately only interesting in their relationship to the whole.

Paul finds nineteenth-century German polymath Alexander von Humboldt particularly interesting, one of whose colleagues was the early brain scientist, Franz Joseph Gall. Gall is the one who developed the idea of functional localization within the brain. At the time, this was a step towards complexity, but over time it has tended to advance a more reductionist mechanical model that Paul rejects. Von Humboldt's view of natural systems has held up better than Gall's. He argued that in the great chain of causes and effects, no single fact can be considered in isolation, and that one must grasp the dynamics of the full web of life in order to understand any one part of it.[3] In this regard, he could be seen as the first complexity scientist. For Paul, the key is that everything affects everything else; the behaviour that arises from these interactions cannot finally be located exactly in any one part of the brain.

The metaphor that appeals to Paul most for this kind of complexity is the murmuration of starlings, an extraordinary phenomenon in which hundreds and thousands of birds swirl and whirl all over the sky in ever-changing patterns. Individual birds can be tracked, but that does not explain the spectacle. Even if, as some think, the birds follow some basic rules – such as: 'avoid being the target of that predator by heading for the thickest mass' – the whole is far more complex than that and not really well understood. In murmuration, Paul sees a clue to understanding our own brains in the repeated, but always different, forms of synchronization, and then desynchronization, that one actually does observe. 'It's about the patterns', he says, 'not about one area, one function. It's about how networks interact, always changing. It's the dynamism of the relationships and interactions that matters. This is what gives us a way to look at the brain as an integrated whole'.[4]

Like Neil Young's search in music for 'the promise of the real', Laurienti desires a richer grasp of mind and not just brain activity. He begins with the contingent complexity of biological existence, specifically human life, with all its wild, hurricane-like character.

How Life Works

To pursue this further, we turn to mycelium, to living organisms that invite us to think freshly about how life works in ways that hint at deep accountability. Mycelium is deep, quite literally, most of it being underground, unseen by us. Neither plant nor animal, it is fungi, a kingdom of its own, as Merlin Sheldrake in *Entangled Life* makes clear, with literally millions of varieties, present everywhere, in every habitat, even inside us. And it can be massive: the largest *single* living organism in the world is the 'Humongous Fungus' in Oregon's Malheur National Forest, almost four square miles in extent. Besides scale, it's not entirely wrong to say that mycelium has a kind of mind of its own too. Its networks of fungal cells, called *hyphae*, branch, fuse, flow and wrap around and under trees and plants that depend upon these mycorrhizal relationships, connecting them and exchanging nutrients, sharing chemical and sometimes even electrical information about what's happening around them.

One aspect of mycelium is probably familiar to all of us. When mycelial networks fruit, they produce a huge variety of mushrooms, some of which we can eat and some not. To be sure, fungi can cause diseases among humans, other animals, plants and trees, but they also give us many powerful medicines, penicillin being one example. Many of them are what Sheldrake calls 'metabolic wizards'[5] who can, for example, decompose our rubbish or even deal with some kinds of plastic in the case of the Oyster mushroom – turning what looks like death into new life by disassembling it into other, usable organic compounds.

Mycelium isn't human, of course. But we can work with it, just as we do with running water or electromagnetic fields, to do creative things. We have discovered that we can use it in clothing and food, guide it to make boxes and packaging, replace plastics with it, build with it in construction, creating fascinating new forms of architecture and design. It can help us with other species, for instance, to act as medicine for bees, which farm and harvest mycelium for their hives. And it promises to be a valuable part of a more energy-efficient, sustainable future. But its greatest gift is a perspective on how we might find our place and be accountable for our role in the world.

There is far more going on under our feet than we think, Sheldrake demonstrates. A practising scientist, he thinks, like neuroscientist Paul Laurienti or musician Neil Young, that we are too fixated on our simplistic mental models. And like Laurienti, he believes that even the familiar term *network* 'has collapsed into a cliché',[6] and that we won't get very much further 'unless we question some of our categories'. His challenge, including to himself, is this:

> I wanted to understand fungi, not by reducing them to ticking, spinning, bleeping mechanisms, as we so often do. Rather, I wanted to let these organisms lure me out of my well-worn patterns of thought, to imagine the possibilities they face, to let them press against the limits of my understanding, to give myself permission to be amazed – and confused – by their entangled lives.[7]

So, let's question some of our categories, then. Although we need to be careful not to anthropomorphize nature, mycelium offers us metaphors that might help us understand better, and perhaps be amazed by, our own entangled lives. Sheldrake warns us, however, against what he calls myco-topia fantasies: 'A mycorrhizal fungus that can keep its various plants alive, is at an advantage: a diverse portfolio of plant partners, ensures it against the death of any of them', but 'shared, mycorrhizal networks aren't always beneficial'.[8] The same is true of us. Plant a human being somewhere; whether that becomes a regenerative event or not is far from sure. The kind of relationships that are possible there will be crucial.

The Intimacy of Strangers, and Those Closest to Us

Natural ecosystems are filled with mycelia fusing or merging with an intimate amalgamation of plant life while retaining their identity. Lynn Margulis, a groundbreaking biologist who studied the processes of gene transfer and combination in living entities, called this 'endosymbiosis'. Through it, new hybrid entities emerge that 'combine the abilities of each' to produce 'composite life-forms', creating what she calls 'cosmopolitan places'. This partnership, a meeting she describes as exhibiting 'the long-lasting intimacy of strangers' in which the whole becomes 'far more than the sum of its parts', generates vitality, introduces a flexibility that is otherwise lacking and creates the conditions for 'entirely new possibilities' that work to enhance the flourishing of all.[9]

Margulis might as well have been describing mycelia. As flexible, living networks that ceaselessly remodel themselves, quite literally bringing about 'change from the roots',[10] mycelia are not only present everywhere but, crucially, in Sheldrake's wonderfully fruitful phrase, they act as 'brokers of entanglement'. He knows, and we know, that applied to human life, this is not a literal but a semantic identification, a metaphor and not a description. Metaphors are not trivial, however, shaping not only our language but also our way of seeing and thinking, including, in this case, about our relationships with other human beings – and other creatures or nature itself.

Think of communities as mycelium, filled with adjacent lives that weave across each other in neighbourhoods, through wider communities and, more often than we realize, beyond even national and international boundaries. Not just across space but in time, down through history. The generational impact of trauma, poverty and exclusion from power is an example, along with its opposite, the inherited benefits of comfort, wealth and inclusion. Another is what we now know through genetic tracing of our ancestors, whose origins often turn out to be quite unexpected and far more diverse than we imagined, weaving in us through the ages.

To recognize how normal these astonishing weaves are helps explain the lives of those we know. A doctoral student of Jim's is a good example; his counter-intuitive history is thoroughly representative of so many people and ultimately iconic. He is a Black South African of Xhosa and Sotho parents, but his first names are Martin de Porres,[11] with absolutely no connection to either of those nations or their languages. Martin is a European name, de Porres that of a Peruvian lay brother of the Dominican Order born of an illegitimate union in Lima in 1579. By Peruvian law, he could not become a full member of the Order – because he was Black, the son of a freed African slave woman. Nonetheless, as a lay Dominican, he became widely known for his extraordinary care of the infirm and the sick, even in the middle of deadly epidemics when no one else dared to offer care. In 1837 he was beatified by Pope Gregory XVI, becoming the first Black saint of the Americas.

Martin's grandfather, it turns out, was a Portuguese man from Mozambique who married a South African woman, and wished the name of that long-ago Peruvian saint to be borne by his grandson. Martin's father, meanwhile, carried the Portuguese surname that became his, now Anglicized. Five hundred years of an intricate set of human connections were embodied in his name.

There's more. Martin's doctoral research was rooted in the area where he grew up, near the hill of Ntabelanga. It was there, the place that white authorities called Bulhoek, that Enoch Mgijima in 1920 gathered his growing group of followers, known as the 'Israelites'. Mgijima was personally influenced by a small church in the United States of America known as the Church of God and Saints of Christ. He now led a prophetic movement of Black South Africans intent on defying the intrusion of colonial rule within the new Union of South Africa by occupying the land, their land actually and setting up communal rule. Government authorities tried hard to get the Israelites to move, but to no avail. A standoff resulted. As time went on, more and more people joined the Israelites from around the country. This was not to be tolerated. In 1921, a large police force armed with machine guns, a cannon and artillery attacked the settlement. One hundred and sixty-three Israelites were killed in what is now known as the Bulhoek Massacre.

Martin had encountered some of the old people who still remembered what had happened to them. They still practised some of the rituals and spoke some of the prayers that were part of that original community of Israelites. Now he wanted to tell a different story than the one long reported in South African history books, of a people of deep values and commitments who resisted White rule, drawing on impulses from the freedom struggle of African Americans in the United States of America and the Hebrew Bible. Mycelium, of the human variety.

Not Afraid of Ourselves

This is not an isolated story. We are all at some level affected by lives that go far beyond our immediate identities. They include many who to us are strangers but whose actions, thoughts and presence in history ripple down through time and across space, sinking into our being in a special kind of intimacy that we barely recognize but never escape. These lives leave knots, lines and traces in us and around us.[12] We awake with surprise to their presence. We can also decide how we respond to this 'intimacy of strangers' – by rejecting it in fear, shame or denial, alternatively, by embracing it and gaining from it in enrichment, joy and expansion. Bringing that breadth of humanity into view can be scary, for we may not know how to cope with 'the other' who is adjacent and different, threatening in their identity or presence.

This is a crucial point. So much of our human history is shaped by fear of the other, whether inside ourselves (when we repress aspects of our self and identity that we don't know how to integrate) or outside of our familiar circles (when we fight or flee from the other who encounters us with a demand we find hard to integrate). Ultimately, however, we cannot escape the direct or indirect presence of the other.[13]

There is, then, a humbling nature to our wildly complicated human family story. Its historical entanglements are so complex that they are almost untellable, often barely making sense if we stick to our standard ways of defining ourselves. Our new ability to decode and trace the history of the human genome makes one thing clearer: not only are we far more shaped than we usually assume by extraordinary kinds of human encounters, some of which reach back so far in time that we can't be sure how they happened though we know they did; we are intrinsically a hybrid of these encounters. Any search for ethnic, 'racial' or any other kind of biological or cultural purity as the defining mark of who we are is, in this light, not just a fool's errand; it's an egregious error.

The one who stokes division on these grounds is the one who makes no sense. And the more you know about the human ecosystem, the less sense it makes. To turn our historical entanglements into a claim for one identity against another is almost always a precursor to contempt, hatred and ultimately violence. To recognize and accept them is to liberate us to live forward. It frees us to start with the whole.

Starting with the Whole

Most of us accept that we live in a round world (actually mildly pear-shaped). Yet we might as well be flat-earthers if we don't grasp the human implications. We appear, to ourselves, to be fundamentally separated by geography, nationality, origin, physical features and cultural histories in the same way we think that the horizon of our vision is a defining edge. Yet these nonessential identities – in the sense that they are secondary to what defines us as human – which we think are real, are as misleading as the horizon. There is only a complex us.

Look a little more closely and we find two things to be the case: almost every one of us is a hybrid of many identities across space and through time; and no one is unaffected by what other people have thought and done across millennia of human encounters that span the globe and are now so pervasive that it is hard to untangle any of it. The patterns of our life together are diverse and remarkably regular through our long history,[14] but they are always the product of the same creature with the same fundamental capacities.

The round planet turns us back on ourselves to emphasize an ever-growing involution that links us not just to those close to us but to an intimacy with strangers that we fail to recognize at considerable long-term cost. But it can be terrifying to those who wish only to stay the same by staying apart. Confronted by too many strangers, it feels to them as if the whole planet has left the rails, even if there are essentially no rails and never have been. What we can discern are dynamic patterns that point us towards how to live in the face of complexity rather than simplicity, unafraid of it and trusting life.

Elsewhere, we have labelled these patterns the 'leading causes of life', of which we name five: agency, coherence, hope, connection and intergenerativity.[15] Fully grasped, they are dynamically integrated, inclusive, robust and parsimonious enough to work with at any scale. They take form in and flow through living relationships, each cause reinforcing the others. Aware and respectful of the life of the whole rather than aimed at the exclusionary defence of a part (think nationalism, jingoism, racism and so on), they describe a pattern that constantly drives towards greater vital efficiency.

That's an unexpected word: efficiency. Here, though, it does not refer to any crude arithmetic of simplicity, to zero-sum measures or the extractive calculus that Mazzucato tells us is false value. Rather, we mean the efficiency of living systems in any given time and ecology, which aims at sustained generativity, at flourishing, constantly finding more vital efficiencies through adaptive novelty. That's how life works, and though we are offered no guarantees, it's why we can trust it in radical times when all the rails we thought were there evaporate entirely.

The 'round world' is about a sense that comes from actually living in this complex web of relationships, ones that of course include our relationship to nature or the earth itself from which we have become somewhat alienated through industrialization, urbanization, computerization and other high-tech ways of managing our lives. Intriguingly, where our language is influenced by the ancient Greek notion of the *oikos*, we retain a hint of an earlier worldview that understood our intimacy with each other, with other species and with nature. The *oikos* is the 'household', originally a holistic concept that incorporated not just the persons who inhabited a home but the animals, crops, land and graves of those who had gone before, along with the sacred hearth, a signifier of spiritual and not just material existence.[16] The words that reference this ancient notion whose meaning we would do well to recover are 'economy' (*oikos nomos*, the custom of the household), 'ecology' (*oikos logos*, the principles or wisdom of the household) and in a religious context, 'ecumenical' (*oikoumené* , 'the world as household').

Crucially, a coherent sense of the whole is also teleological, that is, filled with a sense of purpose and meaning. There is a point to it all, to living generatively with care and conviction, oriented towards what is possible and not just trapped in the actual or the way things happen to be. Nothing ensures us that this will play out as we hope (empirical evidence might even persuade us otherwise), and we have no external guarantees that it is worth 'walking' in ways that express this hope. What we do have, as a potential in us, is a set of inherent and dynamic capacities upon which we can draw and live out in service of the whole, our eyes, heart and mind focused not just on the actual but also on the possible. And, as our discussion of capacities in an earlier chapter makes clear, this is no abstract matter. We are crippled in our daily work if, constrained entirely by the actual, we don't understand what is possible.

Involution, as inevitable and potentially generative as evolution, points us towards the way we humans find our way towards each other as part of the large natural systems that define our opportunities and possibilities. How we turn towards each other, however, matters. Sometimes it results in anxiety, tension and the pressures of social conflict that explode into angry political venom. On our small planet, in our time, it may be important for us to see that turning towards each other as a phase of life finding its way is what matters most.

We are thereby invited to form and re-form our relationships constantly as we walk, even as our ways of walking are also far from simple or obvious. They too are part and parcel of the complexity of life for which we are called to be deeply accountable, and this is the theme to which we now turn.

Notes

1 Merlin Sheldrake, *Entangled Life: How Fungi Make Our Worlds, Change Our Minds & Shape Our Futures* (Random House, 2020), 138–9.
2 David Samuels, 'Neil Young's Lonely Quest to Save Music', *New York Times Magazine*, 22 August 2019.
3 See Andrea Wulf, *The Invention of Nature: Alexander Von Humboldt's New World* (Knopf Doubleday, 2015), especially chapters 17–18 on 'Evolution and Nature' and 'Humboldt's *Cosmos*'.
4 Personal conversation.
5 Sheldrake, *Entangled Life*, 10.
6 Ibid., 72.
7 Ibid., 27.
8 Ibid., 163–4.
9 Ibid., 85–7.
10 Ibid., 190.
11 Last name withheld.
12 See Chapter 7, 'Walking', for our discussion of the idea of meshworks.
13 Both Emmanuel Lévinas and Paul Ricoeur address these realities, Levinas in *Totality and Infinity: An Essay on Exteriority* (Duquesne University Press, 1969), and Ricoeur in *Oneself as Another* (University of Chicago Press, 1992), Levinas insisting that our encounter with the other as judge is the foundation of all moral action, Ricoeur arguing that the self is always already constituted by the other as another.
14 David Graeber and David Wengrow, *The Dawn of Everything: A New History of Humanity* (Farrar, Straus and Giroux, 2021), building on extensive research into our origins

to powerfully demonstrate this regularity in challenging the widespread notion that humans moved through time in a straight line of development.

15 Gary R. Gunderson and Larry Pray, *Leading Causes of Life* (The Center of Excellence in Faith and Health, Methodist Le Bonheur Healthcare, Memphis, 2006); Gary R. Gunderson and James R. Cochrane, *Religion and the Health of the Public: Shifting the Paradigm* (Palgrave MacMillan, 2012), 59–79. See also: http://www.leading-causes.com/about-lcl.html.

16 This is virtually identical to the Xhosa concept of *iKhaya* and its analogues in other southern African Nguni languages; see Vuyani Vellum, 'The Quest for *Ikhaya*: The Use of the African Concept of Home in Public Life' (Master's Dissertation, University of Cape Town, 2002).

Chapter 7

WALKING

Knots or bundles of relations,
Spreading in multiple directions,
Entangled, some stronger or weaker,
With more or less presence, thicker or thinner,
Ever-changing traces

In the Arctic the rivers flowing from the Brooks Range near the cold sea slow and spread into a complex weave of shallow currents surrounded by tundra. For thousands of years this severe land has been the nursery of the caribou, who risk wolves and bears to come here to give birth to another generation. They don't stay long, as the clouds of mosquitoes chase them and their baby calves back towards the high mountains.

The rare human eye sees the tundra stretch as a seamless flat green carpet leading up to the treeless shelves before the rocky foothills. It is not easy walking for a human, as the grassland lives on a thin bit of soil on top of permanent ice only a few feet below. It's wiser to follow the caribou who have, over thousands of years, marked a complex mesh of trails. The young caribou trace not one narrow path, which would make it too easy for the wolves. They follow – and in the process regenerate – a mesh of trails, so that the entire herd moves as a whole from their Arctic nursery to the high ground and then back again as they have done across the millennia.

The caribou give another herd animal – us – a powerful model of how to move together without the dangerous simplicities we tend to live by. If Jesus had come to the Arctic, not the Mideastern desert, he might have spoken of the caribou instead of the biblical camel and the eye-of-the-needle or shepherd and lamb metaphors. We might have religious directions more suited to the complex round planet on which we have to find our way.

The perfectly adapted caribou force the question: For what are we humans adapted? For simplicity or complexity? What capacities help us move as both caribou and humans navigate rapidly changing terrain? Tim Ingold is an anthropologist who studied the caribou of north-eastern Finland and the

Skolt Sámi people who live with them, focusing on the human–animal relations.[1] He realized, contrary to expectations, that the way humans engaged
with the whole complex ecology, including animals, followed no fixed lines.
Even purportedly stable nodes of contact regularly dissolved and reformed.
Rather than the computer-based metaphor of *networks* to describe these complex connections, Ingold suggests we follow the caribou in seeing our connec-
tional reality as 'meshworks'.

'Meshworks': Lines, Knots, Traces and Leaks

If you look up 'meshwork', you will usually be told it's a synonym for 'network'. This seems close enough to not bother with the difference, but men-
tally we tend to think of networks in too linear a fashion, stripping out crucial
nuance and making all subsequent work harder. Ingold holds that the idea of
a network, typically consisting of nodes and connecting pathways, 'flattens
out' the world too much, specifically in the process obscuring power structures and inequalities.[2] By his term 'meshwork' he means something subtly,
but profoundly, different.

Ingold was raised to see complexity on the hoof because, like Sheldrake,
his father was a mycologist who saw it everywhere. Not unlike mycelial webs,
Ingold sees in the walking of caribou a pattern of life marked by intersecting
lines of interaction that are multidirectional and dynamically knotted rather
than flat and nodal. They represent 'knots or bundles of relations, spreading
in multiple directions, able to entangle each other, some stronger or weaker,
with more or less presence, creating thicker or thinner but ever-changing
traces.'[3]

As twenty-first century moderns, we usually think of our places being
organized as relatively fixed hubs, with connections that radiate out from
them and back in again. Ingold calls this a 'hub and spoke model' of reality.[4]
But the idea of a fixed hub hides the living dynamic phenomenon we actually
experience. Far from simple or relatively static, our relationships are living
threads, full of movement, entangling each other in knots, ones that unravel
through time and knot again in new ways, tightly or loosely, trailing other
lines with them, often generating unexpected connections and interactions
where one did not expect them. Seen this way, we do not live in 'places' but in
dynamic 'zones of entanglement'.

Take a hospital, often described as the 'hub' of a wider healthcare delivery
system that are like lines moving in and out from the centre. You can locate
the hospital on a map and describe its architecture, say what's in its walls
and what not, decide what should happen inside its 'place', and choose to

treat anything outside it as extraneous. As far as it goes, that seems appropriate, even normal. But this is a reductionist view of the place of a hospital in the health of a people. The description of it as a mere hub lacks crucial nuance about how the complex mesh of knots and pathways in and out of it function. That, in turn, leads to simplistic planning and implementation. Consequently, people die, or at least fall far short, of what science knows is possible. Thinking with the wrong metaphor can be almost as faulty as the thinking of what we called the financial acolytes of corporate healthcare. Illich wants us to do better than that.

From a meshwork perspective, the hospital represents only a moment in the life journey, through which flow the lifelines of people and things, as well as a plethora of ideas and concepts, all knotted together, sometimes productively, sometimes unravelling. Everything that contributes to this knotting, human and non-human, animate and inanimate, internal and external, is a legitimate part of its zone of entanglement. The hospital – in particular, its purpose of delivering health and attending illness and disease – is never separate from the threads of engagement that spread in multidirections, trailing unexpected ends that shift and change the reality one is dealing with. The hospital, then, is itself knotted into – directly implicated in – the health of persons and communities, not merely a place to which one goes when one must that otherwise has no connection to the life beyond it. Put differently, to think of the hospital merely, or even primarily, as the defining core of a health system is cut off one's view of the whole, potentially to the point of harm.

Ingold adds a further nuance to the idea of a meshwork; it 'leaks'. As he puts it, 'the lives of things generally extend along not one but multiple lines, *knotted together at the centre but trailing innumerable "loose ends"* at the periphery [...] no longer a self-contained object, the thing now appears as an ever-ramifying web of lines of growth'.[5] Here there are no concrete, external boundaries that keep some things (or people) out and others in. In reality, the threads trail beyond themselves and get caught in other threads, 'forever discharging through the surfaces that form temporarily around them', stretching into a past that continues to pulsate into the present and shapes the possibilities of the future too. For us human beings, all of it comes together in 'the social as the domain of their entanglement'.

An Intellectual Meshwork

One may read history through a hub-and-spoke network model, too, rather than as a meshwork, in the process hiding how things have come to be and making us less likely to imagine what might happen next. Consider, for example, a definitive and consequential piece of the history of post–World War II healthcare, to which we have already alluded.[6]

It began with an influential group of people with wide experience of medical missions around the world and high international profiles in the field of health and medicine, who met in Tübingen, Germany, in the mid-1960s. They were concerned about one thing above all: The lack of adequate healthcare for vast numbers of people around the world. They had recognized that they were dealing with a major problem, governed by too narrow a view. Though they were proud of the frequently outstanding, if not world-class, mission hospitals in many parts of the world with which many of them were linked, they also saw something else: That these facilities were great at serving those who could access them but that they had very little impact on the health profile of the wider community within which they were located.

In response, they initiated and led the Christian Medical Commission under the auspices of the World Council of Churches in Geneva. They set about holding local consultations and looking for models wherever they could find them around the world that would inform a different approach. They sought the threads and traces, the trailing ends connecting with each other that lay outside of formal medical facilities but were the way into the existence of the community. Thinking more like a meshwork, informed by multiple new ideas such as the barefoot doctor, and chastened by warnings from people like Ivan Illich of the 'medical nemesis' that would be evoked by centralized, specialized and costly healthcare often difficult to access, they advocated for what we now know as primary healthcare. Halfdan Mahler, then head of the World Health Organization (WHO), took particular interest, feeding their insights directly into the WHO. From this emerged the mantra 'Health for All' that became the mandate of the WHO through the Alma-Ata Declaration of 1978.[7]

The situation is not much different in all too many places today, not least in some of the most affluent countries of the world where you would expect something else. Health-for-all is far from being realized. It may even be getting worse as general practitioners (GP) disappear from villages and small towns while healthcare facilities fill up with specialists. Not only does one lose the knowledge of personal histories and circumstances that a good GP would have; now the burden of first direct interactions with someone who needs help falls on those who work in a stressed emergency room at a facility where strangers deal with the person. Meanwhile the cost of secondary and tertiary healthcare and of medicines grows, almost exponentially, burdening the whole even more. This is the hub-and-spoke model raised to deadly scale, a 'way of walking' towards death not life, made inevitable by a flawed way of thinking.

The failure of the hub model imperils more than the general practitioners, however, whose disappearance could conceivably be compensated in part (but only in part) by virtual electronic consultation and delivery technologies. The idea of the hub concentrates the money, the training, the deliverables and the power in clinical and medical facilities despite the fact that the life-long journey of health for persons and communities depends on lines, knots and traces – meshworks – that thread into but mostly lie outside of such facilities (for the vast majority merely temporary stopping places on that journey). What lies outside the hub gets far less attention and intelligence and is treated as outside the competence of medicine and healthcare. Seeing it as someone else's problem, we define it away using such flawed metaphors as 'upstream' (all the external, social causes health that throw people into the stream of illness and disease) and 'downstream' (where people are hauled out of that stream to be treated in a facility) – another version of the hub-and-spoke model and mentality.[8]

This is not how human beings journey through life. We interact dynamically with each other and with the world around us, through time and space, leaving traces of ourselves, of our movement, of our presence. Through it all flow other people, other creatures, things, ideas and discourses in one complex reality of interwoven lines of growth and movement. What we call health is a composite of this reality, dynamic and fluid in nature, built through re-knotting lines and parsing relevant traces both past and present. Ill-health is where vital lines are severed, where growth and movement break down or stop. Biomedicine and all its tools are part of the mesh, as are its facilities, institutions and training that add to the capacities. It's not poetry but an accurate description of reality to see that just as the *whole* system is bound to the full meshwork, so too the *whole* system heals.

'Affective Entanglement'

Any living human meshwork is never just about material, institutional or ideational entanglements. So much of considerable consequence that goes on in human lives has to do with affect, not so much the ephemeral emotional moments or sparks but the durable, if shifting, attachments we build from the womb onwards that shape how and why we act or fail to act. Largely invisible to instrumental, technical, managerial or merely transactional approaches to our institutions, organizations and facilities, affections may well be decisive in organizational function.

In research we undertook for the WHO in Zambia through the African Religious Health Assets Programme, we saw just how this could play itself out. We focused on identifying and including all those human assets relevant to the health of communities in particular areas. Sharply aware of structural and political dynamics, we developed a highly nuanced technique of community asset mapping.[9] In Ndola, about two dozen men and women from the local community gathered to explore the question of what local assets, tangible and intangible, were already available to them that they could or did leverage for their health and well-being. We asked them to draw on large sheets of paper a map of their community that identified which assets they valued and why. One group of men and one group of women set about the task.

Their maps were radically different. Neither they nor we expected the difference to be so stark, and a lively discussion ensued. The places and relationships that mattered to women were not the same as those that mattered to the men, and some of this was obviously a result of role differentiation in households and patterns of work. But in both cases a great deal of what they valued as most important for them was defined not materially but emotionally, psychically and in relation to supportive or sustaining relationships. At work was 'affective entanglement', a term we did not know at the time.

The term comes from anthropologist Thandeka Cochrane, who brings another level of vibrant humanity to the mesh. Influenced by Ingold but working as far from the Arctic as one can get – in subequatorial Africa – she studied local, international and historical power dynamics in the shaping of libraries in Malawi's lake district. In the process she realized that a vital, sometimes decisive component bound up with the establishment of these centres in particular Malawian communities, without which their differences in their use and perceived value could not be grasped, is the making, sustaining and breaking of attachments – personal, communal and social.[10] In each and every case feelings around the use and misuse of power in the encounter and conflict between cultures and interests turned out to be a crucial component of their history and their success or failure. Moreover, the traces of those feelings do not disappear but continue in one form or another into the future. She calls this dynamic 'affective entanglement'.

How does it work? Citing Sara Ahmed, Cochrane notes that 'emotions do things, and they align individuals with communities – or bodily space with social space – through the very intensity of their attachments.'[11] Affects thereby generate 'connections' in which 'emotions work to align some subjects with some others'. In creating these connections, affects also entangle people with other people, places and things in ways that are efficacious and enduring.

Ways of Walking

Our entanglement with people, places and things doesn't simply happens to us. The paths we find ourselves on do not appear out of nowhere. In the words of Antonio Machado,[12]

Caminante, no hay camino
se hace camino al andar

[Fellow traveller, there is no path
The path is made by walking it]

If we do not pay attention to the vital affective entanglements that are there
our 'way of walking' within any group, institution, organization or community of which we are a part or into which we enter is not just limited; it
is flawed and potentially dangerous to others, to the purposes we seek to
fulfil and even to ourselves. Affections have patterns that can be studied as
with other facets of humanity, but they are dynamic, complex, volatile and
ultimately unpredictable, not 'things' we can map, tie down and thereby
control.

The human 'way of walking', then, requires emotional intelligence, cultural sensitivity and open-ended humility. Drawing on the metaphor of
involution we have also invoked the importance of relationships that spread
beyond us, taking us beyond the limits we are otherwise unable to tran-
scend, and of the hybrid entities that emerge through a long-lasting intimacy of strangers to combine the abilities of each in a partnership that is
more than the sum of its parts, capable of generating vitality, introducing
flexibility and creating the conditions for new possibilities that enhance the
flourishing of all.

The caribou laid down paths that generation of generation could follow
through a challenging landscape that needed navigating. The human landscape we traverse is similarly challenging, the paths we make not necessarily
headed towards the good and the right, and many already made perhaps
limiting us in our vision of where we might more profitably go. That last
possibility, which sociologists call path dependence, is all too common in the
institutional dynamics of which we are a part. In the context of the U.S.
health system Ezekiel Emmanuel argues that following the well-worn paths
is a trap, with the system drifting from one short-term decision to the next,
thousands of which end up creating an overall pattern that is far from what it
promises, producing instead a low-performing clutter.[13] That overall pattern,
like the path of the caribou, regenerates itself one footstep (or hoof) at a time,
tracing the familiar and the established. We end up with a fixation on the
paths we know or have made, not seeing all others that surround and cross it,
perhaps because of unexamined power and privilege or because we are resist-
ant to or fearful of what lies beyond.

It is important then to step back and see the larger pattern that has emerged
from all the micro-decisions, as well as the even larger one within which it
sits. That brings us to the question of complex human ecosystems.

Complex Human Ecosystems

Especially helpful for us is the Human Ecosystem Model (HEM) developed by Burch, Machlis and Force in *The Structure and Dynamics of Human Ecosystems*.[14] It may rank far down Amazon's top sellers, but among those who cannot avoid accountability in confronting ecological scale disasters the book is well known and increasingly used as guide.

Built on eighty years or more of a growing understanding of the relationship between the natural environment and our human social systems, it transcends reductionist approaches to embrace complexity. Phenomena we have tended to see in silos or, at best, as adjacent to each other, turn out to be so deeply intertwined that any kind of deep accountability is probably impossible without paying close attention. Strongly congruent with the perspective we advocate on value, involution and meshworks in the face of the storm, it also has practical implications for our ways of walking (from which it may gain). Briefly, here's what matters about the HEM.

Several exceptional incidents of large-scale environmental disasters in recent times have imperilled entire ecosystems over a large geographical area with a consequent loss of animal life and damage to human economic systems. They include, among others, Hurricane Sandy, massive oil spills in Alaska and France, and the huge blow-out of an oil well in the Gulf of Mexico. Necessary emergency responses are one thing, but the problems of environment they created could only be rectified by repairing the structure and dynamics of the whole ecosystem – beginning with the humans. This needed an almost entirely new organizational logic aimed at aligning all relevant components of the ecosystem. It begins with an understanding of the natural ecology, but quickly moves to components of the relevant human systems, almost all of which turn out to be relevant in some way or another.

The scientific teams brought in to deal with these events realized this, so they turned to the HEM. Thoroughly interdisciplinary,[15] it is designed to make sure that nothing essential is left out of the necessary work. Not unlike assembling Ikea furniture, it stresses how critical it is to consider all of the elements, with none allowed to roll out of sight only to prove essential later. It has two key elements: critical resources and the social system, each of which has three components consisting of variables (see Figure 1).

The components of the HEM are dynamically interdependent, indicated by *flows* between the components, six of which are identified.[16] Together with flows from and to other relevant human ecosystems, this makes instantly clear that events or processes in one component have effects on others, with emergent and not entirely predictable outcomes. Unlike Ikea furniture, the model rests on the realization that one is dealing with life systems that, through time

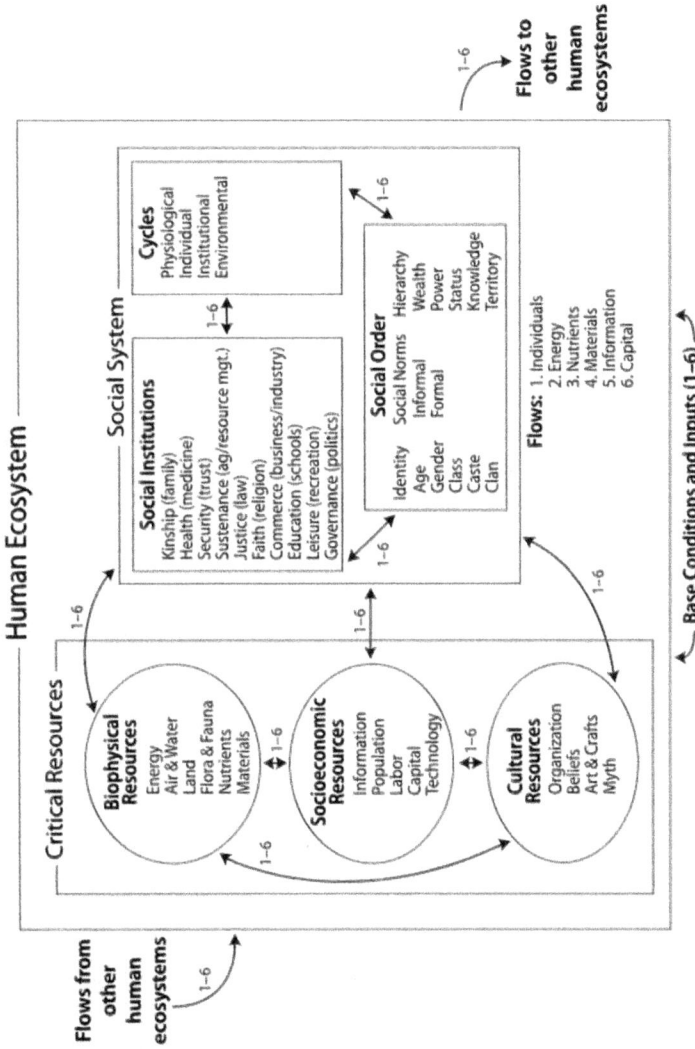

Figure 1 Human ecosystem model.

and space, are 'stochastic, nonlinear, and subject to chaos-induced change and fractal-like complexity'. It is this complex whole that must be grasped.

A particularly important feature of the HEM is its incorporation of cultural resources, social institutions, markers of identity, social norms, hierarchies and the like, that is, of *human agency* and *relationality*. Whereas the authors are clear that physical or material resources are important, 'the nature of what kind of resource it is comes from how specific groups of people sharing a vision of the landscape can reconstruct the meaning of that landscape in many important and significant ways'.[17]

In their chapter on how the HEM was applied in the 276 neighbourhoods of greater Baltimore, for example, they point out that 'In a developing rural area, a tree might be seen as a provider of fuelwood or fodder or sawtimber; in the city, it was the tree's symbolic and social value that was the highest and best use.'[18] They compare this to the GIS system widely used for planning that, as they put it, 'is an excellent guide to gross cluttering and trends in land use and social life', but one that 'often fails to connect with actual information about behavior and hopes'. Further,

> It is often the case that a simple hand drawn map of a district or neighborhood is more helpful in managing crime, responding to environmental crises, or issues of human health. Indeed, it may be of more analytic value than the high-tech, high-elevation map. The more humble map puts less distance between the central authorities and their clients and makes the knowledge of local people a more respected, robust, and effective part of the decision process. The conferring of legitimacy to local knowledge is a critical factor in sustaining cooperative efforts when the central authority is disconnected from communication linkages with local people [...].[19]

This is not marginal to the model; it is central. Effective communication around the values, norms and expectations of the humans who affect the environment – their way of being, thinking and acting – thus becomes crucial to any successful and sustainable ecosystem practice.[20] Far from being secondary, the authors note, because of the impact of our disturbance of nature we humans are a 'keystone species'. One potent indicator of that impact is that human-made things (using plastics, metals, asphalt, bricks, aggregates and concrete) 'now outweigh all forms of natural life'. Citing Robert V. O'Neill's MacArthur Award lecture on the idea of 'ecosystem' (which challenged numerous reductive tendencies in the field), one could even say that 'if there was ever a species that qualified as an invasive pest, it is Homo sapiens.'

Our ways of walking are far from neutral then, the pathways we make through the world and our environment and the direction we choose to take not trivial. Perhaps, as we noted in our chapter on capacities, we do not control the consequences of our decisions, but we can decide how, where and in what direction to walk. O'Neill's somewhat tongue-in-cheek description of us as an invasive pest should not mislead us into thinking that we have no way to think of our presence other than negatively. The idea of an ecosystem, including the HEM, as O'Neill also reminded his listeners, is not an empirical description of nature and our implication in it but 'a paradigm [...], an *a priori* intellectual structure, a specific way of looking at nature'.[21]

We would do very well to include in our way of looking at nature and ourselves a richer understanding of the complex system of which we are part in which involution is at work, in which we grasp the significance of intimate strangers that are made to work towards each other rather than in their little boxes, leaving none out, creating paths that mesh with each other, knotting and unknotting as appropriate, leaving traces that we hope are generative rather than traumatic.

This gives us hope that we can be accountable for the living systems on which all hope rests. It begins with the end in mind: a complex human ecosystem that is alive, dynamic and, most importantly, capable of ongoing adaptive relationship to the larger natural systems, themselves constantly changing. This seems much too hard to *think* about, much less *do*. Surely we can think hard later when we have more time? The deep logic of involution invites us to relax, release our organizational anxiety and accept the invitation to work with the hopeful intelligence of nearly every other species besides our own. We live by moving towards each other – the most natural thing on earth (and probably everywhere else).

Springing Towards Each Other

Involution moves constantly, but usually beneath our consciousness. Human systems occasionally move in fits and starts, sometimes in a life-quake the scale of a global pandemic when nothing can continue in a normal manner. This was the case, for example, when Covid-19 came for us. At the time some of our Leading Causes of Life Fellows were in roles and places where, with others, they could draught a vision of how society (the United States, in this case) could spring from the unknowable damage of the pandemic towards new possibilities for health and wholeness. Thus arose what became the Springboard document, aimed at a path towards comprehensive health.[22]

It focused on 'vital conditions' needed for comprehensive health across a wide spectrum of functional domains like housing, environment, education, employment. As with the HEM, the vital conditions include many moving parts of the system and, at the very centre, from which everything else springs, a domain expressed as 'civic muscle'. Not a functional domain like others, it is the one that gives vitality to all so that the whole ensemble comes alive. Like the HEM, 'vital conditions' is not primarily about a list of problems, but a way of seeing the full array of living assets that can be tended and nurtured to create healthy human ecosystems. That's what we are and can be accountable for, deeply.

This is still a very new way of seeing the future. Covid-19 is not really in our past, yet, and it would be easy to hurry back to the old normal way of seeing and doing things with urgent lists that make programmatic sense, calling for rational budgets optimizing the highest efficiencies. We have seen visions dissolve in such rational acid before (Alma-Ata, for example). We also live in a time when nearly all faith traditions have been to some extent allowed to atrophy and, worse, weaponized like poison in the mesh instead of nectar. Though Thandeka Cochrane does not discuss religious structures, her insights into affective entanglements help us grasp why and how the facets called faith, religion and Spirit are so crucial to the mesh. It helps us see how wrong things can go when the rituals, language, metaphors and practices of faith are captured to serve only part of the mesh and not the whole.

The caribou, Ingold and Cochrane all urge us to think differently about what is possible and how it happens. The 'affective entanglements' of the living mesh are not the inspiring clutter across the street from the real work of organizational work. They are how all social forms function. Some entanglements are stable enough for things that look like institutions to emerge, others moving like the wind through the systems, occasionally blowing them down entirely to clear space for something new. We are caught up in them, we contribute to them and we can work with them. In doing so we take responsibility for what we intend with our lives in the world, not in ignorance of the storm and the judgement of Nemesis but humbly, aware of the intimacy of strangers, attentive to the value of everything and, embracing the power and promise of joy, walking lightly.

Notes

1 Tim Ingold, 'Bindings against Boundaries: Entanglements of Life in an Open World', *Environment and Planning A: Economy and Space* 40, no. 8 (2008): 1796–1810; Tim Ingold, 'Introduction', in *Redrawing Anthropology: Materials, Movements and Lines*, ed. Tim Ingold (Ashgate, 2011), 1–20; Tim Ingold, *Making: Anthropology, Archaeology, Art and Architecture* (Routledge, 2013).
2 Tim Ingold, 'When ANT meets SPIDER: Social Theory for arthropods', in *Material Agency*, ed. C. Knappett and L. Malafouris (Springer Sciences, 2008): 209–15.

3 Tim Ingold, 'Writing Texts, Reading Materials. A Response to My Critics', *Archaeological Dialogues* 14, no. 1 (2007): 35; Tim Ingold, 'Bringing Things to Life: Creative Entanglements in a World of Materials, Paper 15' (ESRC National Centre for Research Methods: Working Paper Series, 2010), 3.

4 Tim Ingold, *Lines: A Brief History* (Routledge, 2016).

5 Cited in Cochrane, 'Epistemic Entanglements', 73.

6 See Chapter 4, section on 'Global Nemesis'.

7 Some of this story appears in Gunderson and Cochrane, *Religion and the Health of the Public*.

8 The upstream/downstream metaphor is too linear to account for the complexity of human health, and wrongly focused anyway. Shifting the metaphor completely, we submit that the stream is not the place of ill-health and disease but represents the journey of life of any one person, family or community, and that medical and clinical facilities are only one side of the bank reaching into the same stream that other agencies on the other side of the bank also reach into. The key is to align both banks simultaneously to keep the stream healthy. See Gary R., Gunderson et al., 'The Watershed of Life: A River Runs Through It', in *Handbook on Religion and Health: Pathways for a Turbulent World*, ed. James R. Cochrane et al. (Edward Elgar, 2024), 444–59.

9 Steve, de Gruchy et al., 'Participatory Inquiry on the Interface between Religion and Public Health: What Does It Achieve and What Not?', in *When Religion and Health Align: Mobilizing Religious Health Assets for Transformation*, ed. James R. Cochrane et al. (Cluster Publications, 2011), 43-61.

10 Cochrane, 'Epistemic Entanglements', 81–4.

11 Sara Ahmed, 'Affective Economies', *Social Text* 22, no. 2 (2004): 119.

12 From Proverbios y Cantares ('Proverbs and Songs') in *Campos de Castilla*, published in 1912.

13 Ezekiel J. Emanuel, *Reinventing American Health Care* (Hachette, 2014).

14 William R. Burch et al., *The Structure and Dynamics of Human Ecosystems: Toward a Model for Understanding and Action* (Yale University Press, 2017).

15 It heads, in fact, in the direction of what Max-Neef called strong transciplinarity; see Manfred A. Max-Neef, 'Foundations of Transdisciplinarity', *Ecological Economics* 53 (2005): 5–16.

16 Ibid., 21.

17 Ibid., 35.

18 Ibid., 152.

19 Ibid., 150–1.

20 Ibid., 32.

21 Ibid.

22 Bobby Milstein et al., eds. *Thriving Together: A Springboard for Equitable Recovery and Resilience in Communities across America* (CDC Foundation, and Well Being Trust, 2020).

Chapter 8

LIGHTNESS

There is a thing I notice in people I love:
An anger – the seeker's anger –
When you see your tribe sitting down
in the middle of the desert
to drink from a mirage,
stuffing themselves with sand
pretending it's water.
What can you do?
Cagn Cochrane[1]

In the end, does the storm consume all? Is nemesis the last word for those we love? Or might this small book of thinking tools help us with our anger at seeing those we love drink from a mirage, settle for eating sand, pretending hope when we know much more is possible and necessary? If our tools are not relevant to that, if our thinking is not strong enough to lead towards life, we will surely continue to drift towards death.

Merely 'rational' decision-making processes based on flawed intellectual principles and simplistic cost-benefit calculations are dangerous. We all do that sometimes and learn the cost again, usually after the damage is done. But we do not always function in narrow self-interest.[2] Sometimes another dimension of our extraordinary capacities of spirit becomes visible and alive. That happens, too.

Theatre of the Soul

We configure and reconfigure the worlds we make and unmake not only through cognition and moral intention but also informed by our experience of beauty, of awe and wonder. Not just an addition to our capacities to under-stand nature (science) or to act towards the highest of which we are capable as a species (morality), it irradiates both science and morality, cohering the oth-erwise incoherent and ultimately pointless and ceaseless flow of appearances as a meaningful and purposive whole. Uniting every aspect of our human spirit, there is no dualism of mind-body in our experience of beauty, of awe and wonder, no fundamental separation of cognition or moral action. Lwando Xaso, a human rights lawyer and writer from South Africa, referencing the South African Constitution, captures this as well as most:

> Art is usually said to be in the domain of the heart and justice is in the domain of the brain. But I think it is mostly women who understand that these two cannot be separated; one enhances the other. *What is the value of art with no justice and what is the value of justice with no art?'* [...] At the core of the Bill of Rights [...] is the respect for human dignity and what holds art and justice together is human dignity.[3]

Shifting the metaphor but keeping the point, we may turn to theatre. We mean specifically what Jim's son, Cagn, trained in theatre and education, calls the 'theatre of the soul', a tricky but productive metaphor.[4] He writes that theatre all too often nowadays is not primarily a creative collaboration, even if artists hope to aim for that. Captured like healthcare, theatre can be a grim corporate exercise, something to be sold and consumed, measured for its worth by the price of the tickets in London's West End, New York's Broadway, Milan's theatre precinct, Cape Town's Foreshore or Tokyo's Shinjuku district. In its soul it is not a show. It is, instead, one of the ways that involution happens in human ecosystems. Quintessentially a 'total craft', one that engages the whole of human experience, theatre

> [...] is physical, it is psychological, it is political, and it is spiritual. It is our oldest form of education, our oldest form of entertainment, our oldest form of therapy, and our oldest form of reflecting on the universe and expressing the human condition.[5]

Theatre and all the arts, including those expressed within religious spaces, hold within them the power to help humans move towards deep accountability. If trapped within a commodified enterprise, however, everyone – the artist, audience and all involved – experiences a fundamental confusion. The relationship between the inner and outer experience of the artist is reversed, generating a chilling structural and systematic contradiction:

> In the public eye one trains and reads and writes and makes work merely as a professional, bowing down to the theorists, the practitioners, the methodologies, the exercises, the career and the industry [...] whilst privately one bows down only to the simplicity of one's yearning, the primal awe of it all, and the need to cry out and to dance.[6]

The contrast is startling. Evident is not only the pain with which so many artists must live, but a desire that bores down into the essence of our humanity. Of what is the awe, for what the yearning? Not the culture of skills that surely is part of one's craft, but a culturing of the human being, of the person as intrinsically of worth, not governed by price or any other external measure.

What can one do, then, when those we love settle for a mere mirage, for eating sand? First, we must not eat sand ourselves. Second, at least one other thing: Turn to the core, re-turn to what grounds our humanity and choose how you will orient yourself in life, to others, to the world as such. Cagn again:

> In the end I can walk across the room to get to the other side, I can walk in a way that makes people want to watch me, or I can walk across the room in such a way that the walking itself becomes a prayer to the gods and perhaps in the end no one can tell the difference.[7]

Why would no one be able to tell the difference between walking and praying? It depends on where and why one is walking. It's not the external act that is decisive but the internal orientation; it's as simple but as profound as that. In this very specific sense, the aphorism that beauty is in the eye of the beholder couldn't be more accurate. Our experience of beauty and awe does not lie in any object out there but in our capacity to embrace the purpose and the mystery of the whole of life as something for which we are deeply accountable. We could also, in language we have used earlier, say that complex human ecosystems are knotted together with affection and beauty, gritty, durable, resilient and generative. That is why life outgenerates death. That is what we are deeply accountable to.

It now also becomes possible to say that the high and gritty work of theatre is the identical high and gritty work of theo-space – all those places in every human culture regarded as sacred within, not apart from, human reality. We see this at the dawn of theatre in Greek architecture in which performance, healing and social-political discourse were all linked, a unity of experience. Similarly, as in a full grasp of the cult of Asclepius,[8] individual illness and recovery were inseparable from the social body, demanding as complex an array of assets aligned with as much nuance and skill as the Human Ecosystems Model or Vital Conditions. Neither of those approaches, the Greeks would caution, will work without deep accountability to beauty and pathos. If we do not move towards beauty and joy, our work is not likely to work at all.

In sum, what we experience as beautiful is not determined by a quality inhering in an external source, but by a quality of a reflective judgement we make and by which we are moved to greater accountability. We respond not just intellectually, but out of a fullness of being that inspires us, that stirs us. We are, in this sense, all artists who must come to terms with what we will and why, and for whom the gaze of the outsider is not the most important element.

It is this quality, this capacity, that unites our drive to explore and understand nature in its fullness with our longing for fullness and the highest good in our relationship to others and to nature itself. It is the bond between curiosity and responsibility. It is simultaneously respect for the profound unity and coherence of nature itself to which we belong, as well as respect for the dignity and worth of all persons no matter what else may distinguish one from the other. Our making and unmaking, if it is to be generative rather than destructive, depends upon this.

Moving Together

Recently, lit by the light of the Milky Way, a group of us held hands to find *our* way through and around a labyrinth set into the rough ground alongside the Peace Grove at Goedgedacht Trust, a bold experiment in rural development an hour and a half north of Cape Town in the Swartland, a farming area just inland from the west coast of South Africa. The Ramadan moon had not yet risen, and the African air was dry enough for the light of the stars to mark the sandstones against the dark gravel.

We moved in towards the centre, then to the left, following the long loop around and out before heading back in and around again. One of us is a Greek scholar. She said we should have been dancing as the Greeks did. We did well enough. Once at the centre, we paused to look up with wonder at the thousands of stars bright against the clear black sky, knowing there are billions beyond our sight and depths far beyond our capacity to imagine, much less grasp. We moved back out, turning, turning, seeking, seeking. Finding our way.

Most find a labyrinth a place of personal way-finding. But holding hands, not quite dancing, this was not personal. It was a hint of a greater whole moving in a social labyrinth. Today it is the whole that needs to find a way, one we are more likely to see by starlight than in the stultifying glow of our electronic screens and their chattering distraction. The deep accountability we seek is not over the horizon beyond sight and beyond our living. It is the path we are already walking.

And while we are not complete, we are enough. The journey, and how we walk together, is the point. We want to be worthy of those relationships; not to be accountable to some abstraction, but worthy of being counted on by those who share the walk. We do not wish to stack ideas like bricks as if doing and making were assembling something from a cosmic Ikea store. Not bricks, but relationships accountable to grow towards each other. The work is the walk, the finding is the seeking; but only together with those we meet on the way.

Wherever there are human beings, the story is also one of courage; not quite fearlessness – for there is much rightly to fear – but of agency and hope, of conviction in favour of the good, the true, the beautiful, of that which gives life even in the midst of all that threatens to take it. This is not illusory, pie in the sky. Everything that needs to happen is already happening in the places and lives we have not yet noticed because we were busy with our own little making and doing. We live in an abundant stream already flowing, not trying to squeeze a little liquid from a parched cactus we found for ourselves.

Still, even with the abundance of partners rising up, it is not clear at all if our combined energies are enough or in time to reverse the planetary processes far advanced that may make human life impossible. We must work in the only way humans can work – with curiosity, joy and creativity – but we must not pause for time is short and the challenges daunting. We must always walk with hands extended to those on the path, much as we did in a labyrinth on the grounds of Goedgedacht.

Good Thinking

Goedgedacht, from Dutch and Afrikaans, means 'good thinking', and it is a good place to see clearly how much good thinking we will all need to find our way. Good trouble is part of it.[9] Here we see radically different lives in a spectrum of whites, blacks and browns speaking far more than the eleven official languages. We also see some of the tensions that are dividing societies everywhere and challenging our attitudes and intentions. The local poor were already poor enough without the arrival of immigrant workers from all over southern Africa now competing for the scarce and difficult jobs. And the local rich were rich enough without finding new ways to exaggerate their privileges.

Our use and misuse of the earth is also invoked. Goedgedacht grows olives from the tough, dry soil to finance the rural development efforts in the villages. However, it can't qualify for the valuable 'organic' label because pesticides drift from the foreign-owned farm next door, which is literally covered in football-sized swathes of plastic to shelter their luxury export crops from the blazing sun. That farm's private dam, shining like a jewel out of place in that bright sun, is filled from a pipe drawing water from a river 15 kilometres away. All this bizarreness is possible because of the speciality grapes and clementines it grows to be shipped abroad. Nothing organic, local or ethical about it. The toxic behaviour drifts.

Only a four-dimensional labyrinth could map the difficulties of navigating such complexity. But that is what the South Africans are doing by the light of the Southern Cross. Shock after shock (AIDS after Apartheid, 'state capture' after freedom, then Covid-19, then […]). Layers of ironic betrayals that would shatter the heart of any lesser people left Mandela, Tutu and, with them, millions of ordinary people who hoped against hope in tears. But the people do not quit. They do not stop putting one foot in front of the next, finding the way by not stopping.

We were at Goedgedacht to convene some of the Fellows of the Leading Causes of Life Initiative. This is a mystifyingly difficult place, like much of South Africa. Life is the only thing tough enough to work here. No simplistic professionalism, no shallow plans, brittle schemes or mere interventions. Only life can live here. Only it can find the way.

How does it do so? By what light? Our hunch is that it might be fuelled by something more like joy, like dance. The word 'joy' falls so short, but still comes closer to the way we move with just enough light to see to the next turn on the path. Not alone, never one by one, always in small groups who would be lost entirely if not held by slender and improbable threads of trust.

At Goedgedacht, one such historical improbability also lights up the sky. Here the Board of the Trust has honoured the memory of the Christian Institute of Southern Africa through a peace grove of now almost forty olive trees commemorating the founding giants who suffered, some of them dying, in the bitter decades of struggle against Apartheid. Built with what we now see as the sinews of life, the Christian Institute defied the massive structures of Apartheid.[10] Nobody involved had any clear thought as to how it could be ended. They gathered and spoke such vivid truth that the government deemed the organization illegal, banned them all, preventing them from being together or even being quoted in public. Tiny, nimble and fragile-looking, they nonetheless persisted, gathering support all across the globe, creating channels for funds to flow into the struggles for justice, dignity and integrity. They eventually won their day in ways that inspire us to struggle with very different demons in ours.

We walk in their light today because they kept weaving thin webs across borders, time zones, political snares, theological lines and impossibilities of every kind. Webs that feed now into the ones we inhabit. Like the Milky Way constellations, the dozens whose names we know reflect millions whom we do not know, who also risked everything for a future that drew them beyond the possible. Most in that movement did not get an olive tree memorial garden, not even a footnote.

What do we do with this light? Their specific answer and ways of strug-gling at that time and in that place are not ours. It is also unlikely they were any smarter than us. Or that they would be any better than we at figur-ing out how to move through the current labyrinth of collapsing climate with political systems so easily gamed and tamed by the cynical powers. Nonetheless ....

We are here now, not them. We are in our struggle, which is not exactly theirs. Their problem was national with some hope to be found abroad. Ours is planetary with no help on the way at all, except for the next generation. They are rising quickly, but time is short.

What can we learn except, like them, to act as best we can: to risk as wisely and boldly as they did with those they trusted with their lives, and with the life of their hopes. Neither they nor we could know if our very best would be enough or in time. Who can ever know that?

You, like us, are already on the way. We want nothing more than to encour-age you to live more fully into what you already grasp and see. Not easy in the face of so much anxiety, perhaps even despair. Not certain knowing that we do not control events. Challenging when one is aware of the aggressive forces of self-interest around us that are neither idle nor weak.

Yet we will fail if all that drives us is dread, despair, doubt or distrust. We will burn out if we no longer know how to celebrate the good, the beautiful and the magisterial. We will be crushed if we forget how to be fully human even as we contend with death.

So, then, hold hands with a few you trust and put one step in front. Turn, move, turn again and yet again, grateful for the light of billions of stars.

Notes

1 Personal communication.

2 Clearly, some people see the world only in terms of exchange relations and consist-ently choose to follow their self-interest above all else; our wager is not on the worst of what we are capable of being but on the best and the highest – equally possible and evident in human experience.

3 Mark Heywood, '"Beauty is a Basic Human Need" – Talking About Art, Justice and Joy', *Daily Maverick*, 14 September 2022, https://www.dailymaverick.co.za/article/2022-09-14-beauty-is-a-basic-human-need-talking-about-art-justice-and-joy (emphasis in the original).

4 'Soul' does not mean some thing or an essence separate from mind-body, but is best understood as a metaphor for the spiritual or immaterial dimension of the human being; see McGaughey and Cochrane, *The Human Spirit*.

5 Cagn Cochrane, personal communication, September 2024.

6 Ibid.

7 Ibid.

8 Bastienne Klein, 'The Ought That Lies Within', in *Handbook on Religion and Health: Pathways for a Turbulent Future*, ed. James R. Cochrane et al. (Edward Elgar Publishing, 2023), 379–95.

9 We echo here John Lewis: 'Do not get lost in a sea of despair. Be hopeful, be optimistic. Our struggle is not the struggle of a day, a week, a month, or a year, it is the struggle of a lifetime. Never, ever be afraid to make some noise and get in good trouble, necessary trouble'; see Joshua Bote, '"Get in Good Trouble, Necessary Trouble": Rep. John Lewis in His Own Words', *USA Today*, 19 July 2020, https://www.usatoday.com/story/news/politics/2020/07/18/5464148002.

10 For the history of the Christian Institute, see Walshe, *Church Versus State in South Africa*.

BIBLIOGRAPHY

AFL-CIO. 'Highest-Paid CEOs'. Accessed 10 December 2024, at https://aflcio.org/executive-paywatch/highest-paid-ceos.

Ahmed, Sara. 'Affective Economies'. *Social Text* 22, no. 2 (2004): 117–39.

Bartz, Tim, Christoph Giessen, Marc Pitzke, Michael Sauga, and Thomas Schultz. „Die feudalistische Welt der Superreichen"' (trans. 'The feudalistic world of the super-rich'), *Der Spiegel*, 20 May 2022, No. 21.

Bauman, Zygmunt. *Liquid Modernity*. Polity Press, 2000.

Bauman, Zygmunt. *Liquid Love: On the Frailty of Human Bonds*. Polity Press, 2003.

Bauman, Zygmunt. *Liquid Times: Living in an Age of Uncertainty*. Polity Press, 2006.

Bote, Joshua. '"Get in Good Trouble, Necessary Trouble": Rep. John Lewis in his Own Words'. *USA Today*, 19 July 2020. https://www.usatoday.com/story/news/politics/2020/07/18/5464148002.

Burch, William R., Gary E. Machlis, and Jo Ellen Force. *The Structure and Dynamics of Human Ecosystems: Toward a Model for Understanding and Action*. Yale University Press, 2017.

Chipkin, Ivor, Mark Swilling, Haroon Bhorat, Mzukisi Qobo, Sikhulekile Duma, Lumkile Mondi, Camaren Peter, et al. *Shadow State: The Politics of State Capture*. Wits University Press, 2018.

Claassens, L. Juliana. 'Tragic Laughter: Laughter as Resistance in the Book of Job'. *Interpretation: A Journal of Bible and Theology* 69, no. 2 (2015): 143–55.

Cochrane, Thandeka J. S. '"The Village" as Entangled: An Exploration of Rural Libraries in Northern Malawi'. *Etnofoor* 31, no. 2 (2019): 87–102.

Cochrane, Thandeka J. S. *Epistemic Entanglements in an Age of Universals*. University of Cambridge, 2020.

Cueto, Marcos. 'The Origins of Primary Health Care and Selective Primary Health Care'. *American Journal of Public Health* 94, no. 11 (November 2004): 1864–74.

de Gruchy, Steve, James R. Cochrane, Jill Olivier, and Sinatra Matimelo. 'Participatory Inquiry on the Interface between Religion and Public Health: What Does It Achieve and What Not?' In *When Religion and Health Align: Mobilizing Religious Health Assets for Transformation*, edited by James R. Cochrane, Barbara Schmid and Teresa Cutts, 43–61. Cluster Publications, 2011.

Emanuel, Ezekiel J. *Reinventing American Health Care*. Hachette, 2014.

Galarneau, Charlene. 'King's Words on Health Injustice: What Did He Actually Say?' *Official Blog: International Journal of Feminist Approaches to Bioethics*, 19 April 2018. https://www.ijfab.org/blog/2018/04/kings-words-on-health-injustice-what-did-he-actually-say/.

Glenny, Misha. *McMafia: Seriously Organized Crime.* Vintage Books, 2009.

Graeber, David, and David Wengrow. *The Dawn of Everything: A New History of Humanity.* Farrar, Straus and Giroux, 2021.

Gunderson, Gary. 'Theogenerative Life and Practice'. In *Handbook on Religion and Health: Pathways for a Turbulent World*, edited by James R. Cochrane, Gary R. Gunderson and Teresa Cutts, 97–112. Edward Elgar Publishing, 2024.

Gunderson, Gary R., and Larry Pray. *Leading Causes of Life.* The Center of Excellence in Faith and Health, Methodist Le Bonheur Healthcare, Memphis, 2006.

Gunderson, Gary R., and James R. Cochrane. *Religion and the Health of the Public: Shifting the Paradigm.* Palgrave MacMillan, 2012.

Gunderson, Gary R., Teresa Cutts, and James R. Cochrane. 'The Watershed of Life: A River Runs through It'. In *Handbook on Religion and Health: Pathways for a Turbulent World*, edited by James R. Cochrane, Gary R. Gunderson, and Teresa Cutts, 444–459 . Edward Elgar Publishing, 2024.

Habermas, Jürgen. *The Theory of Communicative Action Vol. 2: Lifeworld and System: A Critique of Functionalist Reason.* Translated by Thomas McCarthy. Beacon Press, 1987.

Haidt, Jonathan. *The Righteous Mind: Why Good People Are Divided by Politics and Religion.* Vintage Books, 2013.

Hawken, Paul. *Blessed Unrest: How the Largest Movement in the World Came into Being, and Why No One Saw It Coming.* Viking Press, 2007.

Herman, Arthur. *How the Scots Invented the Modern World: The True Story of How Western Europe's Poorest Nation Created Our World and Everything in It.* Crown, 2001.

Heywood, Mark. '"Beauty is a Basic Human Need" – Talking About Art, Justice and Joy'. *Daily Maverick*, 14 September 2022. https://www.dailymaverick.co.za/article/2022-09-14-beauty-is-a-basic-human-need-talking-about-art-justice-and-joy.

Horton, Richard. 'Offline: A New Revolution for Child and Adolescent Health'. *The Lancet* 399, no. 10336 (30 April 2022): P1679. https://doi.org/10.1016/S0140-6736(22)00739-5.

Illich, Ivan. *Tools of Conviviality.* Harper and Row, 1973.

Illich, Ivan. *Medical Nemesis: The Expropriation of Health.* Calder & Boyars, 1975.

Ingold, Tim. 'Writing Texts, Reading Materials. A Response to My Critics'. *Archaeological Dialogues* 14, no. 1 (2007): 31–8.

Ingold, Tim. 'When Ant Meets Spider: Social Theory for Arthropods'. In *Material Agency: Towards a Non-Anthropocentric Approach*, edited by Carl Knappett and Lambros Malafouris, 209–15. Springer Science+Business, 2008.

Ingold, Tim. 'Bindings against Boundaries: Entanglements of Life in an Open World'. *Environment and Planning A: Economy and Space* 40, no. 8 (2008): 1796–810.

Ingold, Tim. 'Bringing Things to Life: Creative Entanglements in a World of Materials, Paper 15'. ESRC National Centre for Research Methods: Working Paper Series, 2010.

Ingold, Tim. 'Introduction'. In *Redrawing Anthropology: Materials, Movements and Lines*, edited by Tim Ingold, 1–20.. Ashgate, 2011.

Ingold, Tim. *Making: Anthropology, Archaeology, Art and Architecture.* Routledge, 2013.

Ingold, Tim. *Lines: A Brief History.* Routledge, 2016.

Jonas, Hans. *Das Prinzip Verantwortung: Versuch einer Ethik für die Technologische Zivilisation.* Suhrkamp Verlag, 1979.

Jonas, Hans. *The Imperative of Responsibility: In Search of an Ethics for the Technological Age.* University of Chicago Press, 1985.

Kant, Immanuel. *Critique of Pure Reason*. Translated by P. Guyer and A.W. Wood. Cambridge University Press, 1998.

Klein, Bastienne. 'The Ought That Lies Within'. In *Handbook on Religion and Health: Pathways for a Turbulent Future*, edited by James R. Cochrane, Gary Gunderson, and Teresa Cutts, 379–395. Edward Elgar Publishing, 2023.

Kristof, Nicholas. 'Good News: Karlo Will Live'. *New York Times*, 6 March 2008. https://www.nytimes.com/2008/03/06/opinion/06kristof.html.

Lévinas, Emmanuel. *Totality and Infinity: An Essay on Exteriority*. Translated by Alphonso Lingis. Duquesne University Press, 1969.

Marquardt, Andrew. 'CEO Pay is Skyrocketing as the Average Worker Struggles to Keep Up with Inflation. Here's Who Got the Biggest Rises'. *Fortune*, 4 April 2022. https://fortune.com/2022/04/04/median-ceo-pay-amazon-discovery-raises.

Max-Neef, Manfred A. 'Foundations of Transdisciplinarity'. *Ecological Economics* 53 (2005): 5–16.

Mazzucato, Mariana. *The Value of Everything: Making and Taking in the Global Economy*. Hachette, 2018.

McGaughey, Douglas R., and James R. Cochrane. *The Human Spirit: Groundwork*. SUN Press, 2017.

McGilvray, James C. *The Quest for Health and Wholeness*. German Institute for Medical Mission, 1981.

McKibben, Bill. *Deep Economy: The Wealth of Communities and the Durable Future*. Henry Holt, 2007.

Meadows, Donella H., Dennis L. Meadows, Jørgen Randers, and William Behrens. *The Limits to Growth: A Report for the Club of Rome's Project on the Predicament of Mankind*. Universe Books, 1972.

Meadows Donella. 'Dancing With Systems'. *The Donella Meadows Project: Academy for Systems Change*, 2002. https://donellameadows.org/archives/dancing-with-systems.

Milstein, Bobby, Monte Roulier, Christopher Kelleher, Elizabeth Hartig, and Stacy Wegley, eds. *Thriving Together: A Springboard for Equitable Recovery and Resilience in Communities across America*. CDC Foundation, and Well Being Trust, 2020. https://thriving.us/wp-content/uploads/2020/07/Springboard-Main-Narrative-For-Screen-2.pdf.

Müller, Tobias, and Thandeka Cochrane. 'Spirituality, Health and Ecology: Co-Liberation, the Climate Movement and the Quest for Planetary Health'. In *Handbook on Religion and Health: Pathways for a Turbulent Future*, edited by James R. Cochrane, Gary Gunderson, and Teresa Cutts, 114–132. Edward Elgar, 2024.

New York University. 'The New York Declaration on Animal Consciousness'. *Effective*, 19 April 2024. https://sites.google.com/nyu.edu/nydeclaration/declaration.

Nouwen, Henri. *Here and Now: Living in the Spirit*. Crossroad Publishing, 1994.

Quamman, David. *The Tangled Tree: A Radical New History of Life*. Simon & Schuster, 2018.

Ricoeur, Paul. *The Rule of Metaphor: Multi-Disciplinary Studies of the Creation of Meaning in Language*. Translated by Robert Czerny, Kathleen McLaughlin, and John Costello. University of Toronto Press, 1977.

Ricoeur, Paul. *Oneself as Another*. University of Chicago Press, 1992.

Rilke, Rainer Maria. 'The Beholder (Der Schauende)'. In *Selected Poems of Rainer Maria Rilke*, translation by Robert Bly, 105 . Harper & Row, 1981.

Rosen, Jill. *A New Visualization of Everything on Earth*. Hub, Johns Hopkins University, 5 June 2024. https://hub.jhu.edu/2024/06/05/biocubes-everything-on-earth/.

Samuels, David. 'Neil Young's Lonely Quest to Save Music'. *New York Times Magazine*, 22 August 2019.

Sandel, Michael J. *The Tyranny of Merit: What's Become of the Common Good?* Allen Lane, 2020.

Schrimgeour, Guthrie. 'Inside Mark Zuckerberg's Top-Secret Hawaii Compound'. *Wired Magazine*, 14 December 2023. https://www.wired.com/story/mark-zuckerberg-inside -hawaii-compound.

Sehlikoglu, Sertaç, and Aslı Zengin. 'Why Revisit Intimacy?'. *The Cambridge Journal of Anthropology* 33, no. 2 (2015): 20–5.

Sheldrake, Merlin. *Entangled Life: How Fungi Make Our Worlds, Change Our Minds & Shape Our Futures*. Random House Publishing Group, 2020.

Simon, Matt. 'The Infamous 1972 Report That Warned of Civilization's Collapse'. Interview: Carlos Alvarez Pereira, *Wired Magazine*, 6 July 2022. https://www.wired .com/story/the-infamous-1972-report-that-warned-of-civilizations-collapse.

Snyder, Ross. *Contemporary Celebration*. Abingdon Press, 1971.

Taylor, Daniel C. *Yeti: The Ecology of a Mystery*. Oxford University Press, 2017.

Taylor-Ide, Daniel, and Carl E. Taylor. 'Community-Based Sustainable Human Development'. *UNICEF*, 1995. https://cdn.future.edu/wp-content/uploads/2018/06 /1995-02-community-based-sustainable-human-development.pdf.

Taylor, Daniel C., and Carl E. Taylor. *Just and Lasting Change: When Communities Own Their Futures*, 2nd ed. Johns Hopkins University Press, 2016 [2002].

Vellum, Vuyani. 'The Quest for *Ikhaya*: The Use of the African Concept of Home in Public Life'. Masters Dissertation, University of Cape Town, 2002.

Walshe, Peter. *Church Versus State in South Africa: The Case of the Christian Institute*. C. Hurst, and Orbis Books, 1983.

Wiesel, Elie. *The Gates of the Forest*. Holt, Reinhardt and Winston, 1966.

Wikipedia, 'The Limits to Growth'. https://en.wikipedia.org/wiki/The_Limits_to _Growth.

Wulf, Andrea. *The Invention of Nature: Alexander Von Humboldt's New World*. Knopf Doubleday, 2015.

Yunkaporta, Tyson. *Sand Talk: How Indigenous Thinking Can Save the World*. HarperCollins, 2020.

Zhong, Raymond. 'Geologists Make It Official: We're Not in an "Anthropocene" Epoch'. *New York Times*, 20 March 2024. https://www.nytimes.com/2024/03/20/climate/ anthropocene-vote-upheld.html.

INDEX

www.ingramcontent.com/pod-product-compliance
Lightning Source LLC
Chambersburg PA
CBHW031447280326
41927CB00037B/381